Teacher Resource Copymasters

HOUGHTON MIFFLIN

Math Steps

HOUGHTON MIFFLIN

Boston • Atlanta • Dallas • Denver • Geneva, Illinois • Palo Alto • Princeton

ISBN: 0-395-98305-3

3456789-B-05 04 03 02 01 00

Contents

Assessments 1

The assessment copymasters give you valuable information about your students' prior knowledge, progress, and understanding of new mathematical content.

From the beginning of the year through the end of the year, you can assess students' understanding of mathematical skills, concepts, and vocabulary. Both free-response and multiple-choice tests are provided.

The results of these tests can help you assess whether students have the necessary prerequisite skills and knowledge in order to be successful with this year's materials, whether students are progressing adequately, and whether students have achieved the goals of the mathematics curriculum.

Reteach Worksheets 57

Reteach Worksheets meet the needs of students who require reinforcement of topics or concepts. The step-by-step instruction on each worksheet supports students through the learning process. The Teacher Note at the bottom of each page tells you when to use the Worksheet.

Some Reteach Worksheets review prerequisite skills or concepts for a unit. Students can use these before they begin a unit.

Most Reteach Worksheets support lessons in a unit. In the Student Book, there is a Quick Check feature that appears at the end of many lessons. The Quick Check reviews the lessons you have just covered. If students have difficulty with any of the concepts or skills on the Quick Check, they can use the Reteach Worksheets that correspond to the items. References to Reteach Worksheets appear in the Teacher Edition in both the Annotated Student Book pages and in the Lesson Support.

Extension Worksheets cover a variety of mathematical content. They give students an opportunity to extend the topic they are learning or they introduce students to new topics.

The Extension Worksheets are organized by unit. The Teacher Note at the bottom of each page tells you when to use the Worksheet. References to Extension Worksheets appear in the Lesson Support in the Teacher Edition.

Teaching Resources are copymasters for frequently used teaching aids and for Family Projects. You may use the teaching aids during the presentation of a lesson or reproduce them for students to use individually. Family Projects provide suggestions for students and their families to work together on the skills and objectives in each unit.

Answer Keys include answers for all of the assessments, as well as the Reteach Worksheets and Extension Worksheets.

Assessments

NOTES

Assessment Overview

At the Beginning of the Year

- **Beginning of the Year Inventory**

  Before your students start Unit 1, you may give them the Beginning of the Year Inventory. This pretest shows whether students possess the necessary prerequisite skills and knowledge to be successful with this year's mathematics.

  You can also use the Inventory as a placement test for students who transfer to your school during the schoolyear.

  The Inventory uses free-response format to test objectives that cover skills, concepts, problem solving, and vocabulary.

Before Each Unit

- **Unit Pretest**

  Assessing prior knowledge helps you build effective lessons using what students already know. You will quickly learn which skills, concepts, and vocabulary your students need to review before they begin a new unit.

  By using the results of the Unit Pretests, you can prepare your students to be confident and successful with the mathematics in the new unit.

During Each Unit

- **Quick Checks in the Student Book**

  Monitor and assess students' progress at regular intervals. The Quick Check reviews the lessons you have just covered.

  References to the Reteach Worksheets and the Skills Tutorial appear in the Teacher Edition in both the Annotated Student Book pages and in the Lesson Support.

After Each Unit

- **Unit Posttest**

  Each Unit Posttest is an additional tool you may use to assess students' mathematical understanding and application of the work in that unit.

  The Unit Posttests are formatted like the Unit Reviews in the Student Book and cover all unit objectives.

At Midyear

- **Midyear Test**

  The Midyear Test covers objectives from Units 1 through 6 in the Student Book. Test results will show which skills or concepts you need to review with students.

  This test is in standardized format to provide your students with valuable experience in taking standardized tests. Students will mark their answers on the answer sheet provided (see Teaching Resource 2) by filling in the space for their answer choice.

At the End of the Year

- **Final Test**

  The Final Test covers objectives from Units 7 through 11 in the Student Book, as well as key objectives from each unit in the first half of the book.

  You can use this summative test to reinforce the topics taught throughout the year and to assess what students have mastered.

  The Final Test is in standardized format to provide your students with more test-taking practice. Students will mark their answers on the answer sheet provided (see Teaching Resource 2) by filling in the space for their answer choice.

Use a word from the word bank to name each figure. Use each word only once.

Word Bank	
hexagon	rectangle
octagon	square
parallelogram	trapezoid
pentagon	triangle

1.

_____

2.

_____

3.

_____

4.

_____

5.

_____

6.

_____

7.

_____

8.

_____

Complete each sentence. Use the number 40,598.

9. The **8** is in the _____ place.

10. The **9** is in the _____ place.

11. The **5** is in the _____ place.

12. The **0** is in the _____ place.

13. The **4** is in the _____ place.

14. Write the number in words. _____

_____

Write the number.

15. eight hundred twenty-six thousand,

three hundred twenty-five _____

16. ninety-three thousand, seven hundred nine _____

17. six million, three hundred thousand,

four hundred eleven _____

18. 60,000 + 4,000 + 300 + 20 + 5 _____

19. 3,000,000 + 500,000 + 80,000 + 900 + 2 _____

20. 1,000,000 + 70,000 + 4,000 _____

Use properties to solve.

21. $7 \times 4 =$ _____ $\times\ 7$

22. $3 \times (4 \times 5) = (3 \times 4) \times$ _____

23. $8 \times$ _____ $= 8$

24. $5 \times$ _____ $= 0$

25. $9 \div$ _____ $= 9$

26. $6 \div$ _____ $= 1$

Write the letters of the figures that answer the question.

27. Which figures have four right angles? _____

28. Which figures have no right angles? _____

29. Which figures have at least two sides the same length? _____

Suppose you spin this spinner. Write *certain*, *likely*, *unlikely*, or *impossible* to describe each event.

30. You will spin a **2**. _____

31. You will spin a **1** or a **3**. _____

32. You will spin a **7**. _____

33. You will spin a **1, 2, or 3**. _____

Write the fraction for the shaded part of the figure.

34. _____

35. _____

36. _____

Write the fraction for the shaded part of the set.

37. _____

38.  _____

39. _____

Name _____

Complete to write an equivalent fraction.

40. $\frac{1}{2} = \frac{}{4}$

41. $\frac{2}{3} = \frac{6}{}$

42. $\frac{8}{8} = \frac{}{4}$

Write the letter of the best estimate.

43. How full is the cup? _____

a. $\frac{1}{4}$ **b.** $\frac{1}{2}$ **c.** $\frac{3}{4}$ **d.** $\frac{4}{4}$

44. What part of the circle is

shaded? _____

a. $\frac{1}{5}$ **b.** $\frac{2}{5}$ **c.** $\frac{3}{5}$ **d.** $\frac{4}{5}$

Write a mixed number to describe the shaded part.

45.

_____

46.

_____

Write the decimal for the shaded part of the model.

47.

_____

48.

_____

Complete.

49. 1 ft = _____ in.

50. 100 cm = _____ m

51. 1 yd = _____ ft.

Name _____

Compare the numbers. Write <, >, or =.

52. 235 $\bigcirc$ 352

53. 1,255 $\bigcirc$ 956

54. 31,254 $\bigcirc$ 30,895

Round each number to the nearest ten.

55. 58 _____

56. 722 _____

57. 5,765 _____

Round each number to the greatest place.

58. 17 _____

59. 447 _____

60. 6,742 _____

Use mental math to find each sum.

61. $22 + 6 =$ _____

62. $31 + 9 =$ _____

63. $8 + 17 =$ _____

64. $4 + 84 =$ _____

Add.

65.
$$\begin{array}{r} \$34 \\ + \ 35 \\ \hline \end{array}$$

66.
$$\begin{array}{r} 153 \\ + \ 374 \\ \hline \end{array}$$

67.
$$\begin{array}{r} 1.4 \\ + \ 0.7 \\ \hline \end{array}$$

68.
$$\begin{array}{r} \$3.12 \\ + \ 1.77 \\ \hline \end{array}$$

69.
$$\begin{array}{r} \$ \ .77 \\ 3.40 \\ + \ 4.81 \\ \hline \end{array}$$

70.
$$\begin{array}{r} 56 \\ 108 \\ + \ 356 \\ \hline \end{array}$$

71.
$$\begin{array}{r} 3,521 \\ + \ 2,908 \\ \hline \end{array}$$

72.
$$\begin{array}{r} 7,503 \\ + \ 591 \\ \hline \end{array}$$

Subtract.

73.
$$\begin{array}{r} 73 \\ - \ 16 \\ \hline \end{array}$$

74.
$$\begin{array}{r} 345 \\ - \ 108 \\ \hline \end{array}$$

75.
$$\begin{array}{r} \$4.56 \\ - \ 2.05 \\ \hline \end{array}$$

76.
$$\begin{array}{r} 8,616 \\ - \ 3,282 \\ \hline \end{array}$$

Name _____

Multiply or divide.

77. $3 \times 7 =$ _____

78. $9 \times 5 =$ _____

79. $4 \times 1 =$ _____

80. $16 \div 2 =$ _____

81. $24 \div 4 =$ _____

82. $30 \div 5 =$ _____

83. $48 \div 6 =$ _____

84. $8 \times 8 =$ _____

85. $72 \div 9 =$ _____

86. $3 \times 0 =$ _____

87. $7 \times 10 =$ _____

88. $10 \times 68 =$ _____

Compare the two fractions. Write <, >, or =.

89. $\frac{1}{2} \bigcirc \frac{3}{4}$

90. $\frac{2}{3} \bigcirc \frac{1}{3}$

91. $\frac{4}{5} \bigcirc \frac{4}{7}$

Write the fractions in order from least to greatest.

92. $\frac{1}{4}$ $\frac{1}{8}$ $\frac{1}{2}$ $\frac{1}{1}$

93. $\frac{2}{3}$ $\frac{2}{2}$ $\frac{2}{5}$ $\frac{2}{1}$

_____

_____

Add or subtract.

94. $\frac{1}{3}$ $+ \frac{1}{3}$

95. $\frac{2}{5}$ $+ \frac{1}{5}$

96. $\frac{3}{4}$ $- \frac{1}{4}$

97. $\frac{7}{8}$ $- \frac{3}{8}$

Write each fraction as a decimal.

98. $\frac{3}{10}$ _____

99. $\frac{29}{100}$ _____

100. $\frac{1}{2}$ _____

Divide. Check your answer by multiplying.

101. $4\overline{)31}$

$$\begin{array}{r} \times\ 4 \\ \hline + \\ \hline \end{array}$$

102. $6\overline{)38}$

$$\begin{array}{r} \times\ 6 \\ \hline + \\ \hline \end{array}$$

103. $3\overline{)96}$

104. $8\overline{)848}$

105. $6\overline{)\$12.30}$

106. $2\overline{)\$4.98}$

Multiply.

107. $\begin{array}{r} 22 \\ \times\ 4 \\ \hline \end{array}$

108. $\begin{array}{r} 415 \\ \times\ 3 \\ \hline \end{array}$

109. $\begin{array}{r} \$1.34 \\ \times\ \ \ 5 \\ \hline \end{array}$

110. $\begin{array}{r} 2{,}341 \\ \times\ \ \ 2 \\ \hline \end{array}$

111. $\begin{array}{r} \$3.25 \\ \times\ \ \ 3 \\ \hline \end{array}$

112. $\begin{array}{r} \$4.05 \\ \times\ \ \ 5 \\ \hline \end{array}$

Find the area and perimeter of each figure.

113.

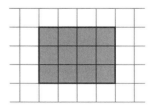

Area: _____ square units

Perimeter: _____ units

114.

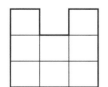

Area: _____ square units

Perimeter: _____ units

Solve.

115. Three candles cost **$.84**. What is the cost of each candle?

_____

116. Osamu had **9** model cars. He got **6** more for his birthday. If he puts the same number on each of **3** shelves, how many models will be on each shelf?

_____

117. Sara has **$25**. If she buys two notebooks for **$3** each, how much money will she have left?

_____

118. Tracy had **345** baseball cards. She bought a package of **25** baseball cards. Then she gave **8** cards to her friend Shannon. How many baseball cards does Tracy have now?

_____

Write the number sentence that can be used to solve each problem. Then solve the problem.

119. A rectangle is **4** inches longer than it is wide. It is **10** inches wide. How long is the rectangle?

_____

_____

120. Leon is twice as tall as his little brother. His brother is **32** inches tall. How tall is Leon?

_____

_____

Use the data from the table to solve.

121. How many more votes did Wolf get than Lincoln got?

_____

122. Who won the election?

_____

123. By how many votes did he win?

_____

Election Results		
Name	**Tally**	**Number**
Yantz	卌 卌 I	
Wolf	卌 II	
Lincoln	IIII	

Write each number in standard form. (1A, 1B)

1. five thousand, seven hundred, twenty-four _____

2. eighty-four thousand, nine hundred seven _____

3. seven hundred sixty-two thousand, eleven _____

4. four million, three hundred thousand, one _____

5. five hundred ninety million, seventy-one thousand,

six hundred ten _____

Write <, >, or = . (1C)

6. 234 ◯ 253   **7.** 8,520 ◯ 8,502   **8.** 5,699 ◯ 5,700

9. 19,000 ◯ 19,100   **10.** 46,363 ◯ 36,663   **11.** 864,452 ◯ 864,452

Round to the nearest hundred. (1D)

12. 344 _____   **13.** 31,216 _____

Round to the nearest ten thousand. (1D)

14. 55,728 _____   **15.** 863,560 _____

Round to the nearest hundred thousand. (1D)

16. 2,721,000 _____   **17.** 8,384,210 _____

The bar graph shows the number of hours Mr. West works in his garden each day. Use the graph to solve. (1E)

18. Look for a pattern in the number of hours Mr. West works in his garden each day. Describe the pattern.

_____

19. Use the pattern to predict the number of hours Mr. West will work in his garden on Saturday.

_____

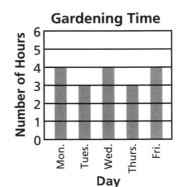

Gardening Time

Write each number in standard form. (1A, 1B)

1. seven thousand, nine hundred seventy-eight _____

2. forty-five thousand, two hundred eight _____

3. three hundred twenty-four thousand, fifty _____

4. eight million, one hundred thousand, six _____

5. nine hundred twenty million, thirty-two thousand,

four hundred twelve _____

Write <, >, or = . (1C)

6. 789 ◯ 759   **7.** 5,406 ◯ 5,460   **8.** 8,800 ◯ 8,788

9. 16,000 ◯ 16,100   **10.** 73,224 ◯ 73,224   **11.** 607,311 ◯ 670,331

Round to the nearest hundred. (1D)

12. 593 _____   **13.** 56,921 _____

Round to the nearest ten thousand. (1D)

14. 49,378 _____   **15.** 348,720 _____

Round to the nearest hundred thousand. (1D)

16. 49,378 _____   **17.** 6,572,300 _____

The bar graph shows the number of days Lisa visited her grandparents each month. Use the graph to solve. (1E)

18. Look for a pattern in the number of days Lisa visits each month. Describe the pattern.

_____

19. Use the pattern to predict how many days Lisa will visit her grandparents in August.

_____

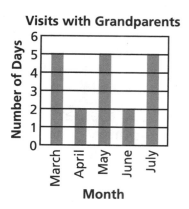

Visits with Grandparents

Name _____

Complete. (2E, 2B)

1. 3 + 5 = 5 + _____

2. 4 + 7 = _____ + 4

3. _____ + 2 = 2 + 9

4. 0 + 14 = _____

5. 0 + 0 = _____

6. 8 + 0 = _____

7. (4 + 5) + 6 = _____ + _____ = _____

8. 4 + (5 + 6) = _____ + _____ = _____

Find each sum or difference. Write the number sentence that shows the inverse operation. (2D)

9. 6 + 4 = _____

_____

10. 13 − 5 = _____

_____

11. 16 − 8 = _____

_____

Estimate each sum or difference by rounding to the greatest place value. (2C)

12.   46 → ___
   + 17 → + ___

_____

13.   619 → ___
   − 288 → − ___

_____

14.   619 → ___
   + 288 → + ___

_____

Add or subtract. (2A)

15.   483
   + 135

16. $56.21
   − 2.61

17.   26,032
   + 4,659

18.   78,000
   − 5,318

Write each amount. Then draw your change. Use the fewest coins and bills. (2F)

19. You have   You spend   Your change

_____   _____   _____

Solve. (2G)

20. Wayne bought a card for **$1.75** and a gift for **$6.50**. Write a number sentence that shows how much he spent.

_____

21. Yuka wants to buy a scarf for **$7.99** and a necklace for **$6.99**. How much change will she get back if she pays with a **$20** bill?

_____

Complete. (2E, 2B)

1. $6 + 5 = 5 +$ _____

2. $9 + 3 =$ _____ $+ 9$

3. _____ $+ 7 = 7 + 8$

4. $0 + 0 =$ _____

5. $0 + 1 =$ _____

6. $17 + 0 =$ _____

7. $(1 + 8) + 6 =$ _____ $+$ _____ $=$ _____

8. $1 + (8 + 6) =$ _____ $+$ _____ $=$ _____

**Find each sum or difference. Write the number
sentence that shows the inverse operation.** (2D)

9. $2 + 5 =$ _____

10. $18 - 9 =$ _____

11. $12 - 8 =$ _____

_____

_____

_____

**Estimate each sum or difference by rounding to
the greatest place value.** (2C)

12. $\begin{array}{r} 78 \rightarrow \underline{} \\ + 32 \rightarrow + \underline{} \\ \hline \end{array}$

13. $\begin{array}{r} 781 \rightarrow \underline{} \\ - 406 \rightarrow - \underline{} \\ \hline \end{array}$

14. $\begin{array}{r} 8{,}771 \rightarrow \underline{} \\ + 4{,}264 \rightarrow + \underline{} \\ \hline \end{array}$

Add or subtract. (2A)

15. $\begin{array}{r} 631 \\ + 287 \\ \hline \end{array}$

16. $\begin{array}{r} \$56.82 \\ - 8.19 \\ \hline \end{array}$

17. $\begin{array}{r} 47{,}860 \\ + 5{,}219 \\ \hline \end{array}$

18. $\begin{array}{r} 33{,}000 \\ - 4{,}832 \\ \hline \end{array}$

**Write each amount. Then draw your change.
Use the fewest coins and bills.** (2F)

19. You have   You spend   Your change

_____   _____   _____

Solve. (2G)

20. Chien bought a model for **$7.95** and glue for **$1.25**. Write a number sentence that shows how much he spent.

21. Marsha is buying a drawing pad for **$5.99** and a set of pencils for **$4.99**. How much change will she get from a **$20** bill?

_____   _____

Use properties to solve. (3A)

1. $(2 \times 2) \times 4 =$ _____
2. $7 \times 0 =$ _____
3. $1 \times 3 =$ _____

Multiply. (3B, 3C, 3E, 3F)

4. 42
      $\times$ 6

5. 62
      $\times$ 3

6. 463
      $\times$ 8

7. 6,214
      $\times$ 4

8. 30×5

9. $3.12
      $\times$ 9

10. $16.45
      $\times$ 5

11. 540
      $\times$ 100

12. 25
      $\times$ 14

13. 367
      $\times$ 22

Estimate the product. (3D, 3E)

14. 76 $\rightarrow$
      $\times$ 4 $\rightarrow$ $\times$ _____
      _____

15. 51 $\rightarrow$
      $\times$ 19 $\rightarrow$ $\times$ _____
      _____

16. $7.82 $\rightarrow$
      $\times$ 48 $\rightarrow$ $\times$ _____
      _____

Solve. (3G)

17. Mike bought two kinds of cat food and a cat bell. One type of cat food cost twice as much as the other. The bell cost **$.50**. Mike spent **$5.00**. How much did each type of cat food cost?

_____

18. Who wrote the most letters?

_____

19. How many letters did Joanne and Amanda write altogether?

_____

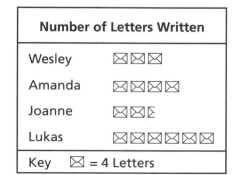

Number of Letters Written	
Wesley	✉✉✉
Amanda	✉✉✉✉
Joanne	✉✉◁
Lukas	✉✉✉✉✉✉
Key	✉ = 4 Letters

Name _____

Use properties to solve. (3A)

1. $(4 \times 2) \times 5 =$ _____   **2.** $6 \times 0 =$ _____   **3.** $1 \times 5 =$ _____

Multiply. (3B, 3C, 3E, 3F)

4. 25
    × 5

5. 94
    × 2

6. 358
    × 4

7. 5,425
    ×   6

8. 40
    × 30

9. $4.13
    ×   4

10. $13.78
    ×   7

11. 80
    × 50

12. 76
    × 24

13. 115
    × 52

Estimate the product. (3D, 3E)

14. 45 →
    × 8 → × _____
    _____

15. 83 →
    × 18 → × _____
    _____

16. $5.29 →
    × 69 → × _____
    _____

Solve. (3G)

17. Dora bought two rings and some wrapping paper. One ring cost twice as much as the other. The wrapping paper cost **$.50**. She spent **$6.80**. How much did each ring cost?

_____

18. How many more books did Priscilla read than Caleb read?

_____

19. How many books did the three students read altogether?

_____

Number of Books Read	
Caleb	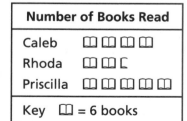
Rhoda	
Priscilla	
Key 📖 = 6 books	

Simplify each expression. (4B)

1. $3 \times (2 + 5)$ _____

2. $42 - 3 \times 4$ _____

3. $3 \times 8 \div 4$ _____

Divide. (4C, 4F)

4. $6\overline{)35}$

5. $4\overline{)337}$

6. $5\overline{)\$7.45}$

7. $3\overline{)2,645}$

Use divisibility rules to solve. (4D)

8. Circle the numbers that are divisible by both **3** and **2**.

   12   15   24   33   60   80

---

9. Circle the numbers that are divisible by both **5** and **3**.

   24   30   42   45   66   90

Complete the box by writing the product with as many different pairs of factors as possible. Circle the prime numbers. (4A)

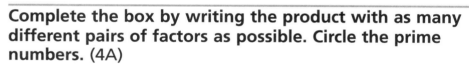

10.   16

11.   32

12.   37

13.   54

Find the average of each set of numbers. (4E)

14. 4, 3, 6, 9, 3 _____

15. 45, 33, 27 _____

16. 56¢, 24¢, 15¢, 25¢ _____

Solve. (4G)

17. The clerk gave Eduard $5 in change when he bought 4 bottles of juice for **$1.25** each. How much money did Eduard give the clerk?

_____

18. Alexis paid **$1.65** including tax for **3** bows. Each bow was the same price. What was the price of each bow?

_____

Simplify each expression. (4B)

1. $5 \times (3 + 6)$ _____

2. $36 - 6 \div 3$ _____

3. $8 \times 5 \div 4$ _____

Divide. (4C, 4F)

4. $9\overline{)52}$

5. $8\overline{)638}$

6. $6\overline{)\$7.32}$

7. $4\overline{)3,377}$

Use divisibility rules to solve. (4D)

8. Circle the numbers that are divisible by both **5** and **2**.

    12   15   30   54   60   80

9. Circle the numbers that are divisible by both **2** and **3**.

    24   36   51   46   66   93

Complete the box by writing the product with as many different pairs of factors as possible. Circle the prime numbers. (4A)

10.   18

11.   63

12.   40

13.   53

Find the average of each set of numbers. (4E)

14. 9, 3, 6, 8, 9

15. 35, 28, 18

16. 28¢, 48¢, 16¢, 32¢

_____   _____   _____

Solve. (4G)

17. The clerk gave Julia **$3.25** in change when she bought **3** cartons of milk for **$2.25** each. How much money did Julia give the clerk?

_____

18. Will paid **$5.25** including tax for **3** magazines. Each magazine was the same price. What was the price of each magazine?

_____

Complete each list of multiples. Circle the common multiples. (5A)

1. Multiples of **4**: **12, 16,** _____, _____, _____, _____, **36,** _____, _____

Multiples of **6**: **12, 18,** _____, _____, _____, **42,** _____, _____, _____

Write an equivalent fraction in simplest form. (5B)

2. $\frac{12}{15}$ _____   **3.** $\frac{6}{18}$ _____

Compare. Write <, >, or =. (5C)

4. $\frac{3}{4}$ ◯ $\frac{4}{5}$ **5.** $\frac{3}{6}$ ◯ $\frac{1}{2}$

Order from least to greatest. (5C)

6. $\frac{5}{6}$ $\frac{1}{2}$ $\frac{3}{4}$ $\frac{1}{3}$ _____

Write each as a fraction. (5D)

7. 3 _____   **8.** $3\frac{2}{3}$ _____

Add or subtract. Write your answer in simplest form. (5E, 5F)

9. $\frac{5}{8}$
$-\frac{3}{8}$

10. $\frac{2}{7}$
$+\frac{3}{7}$

11. $1\frac{1}{5}$
$+2\frac{2}{5}$

12. $4\frac{5}{8}$
$-3\frac{3}{8}$

13. $\frac{1}{4}$
$+\frac{3}{8}$

14. $\frac{3}{5}$
$+\frac{3}{10}$

15. $\frac{5}{6}$
$-\frac{1}{3}$

16. $\frac{7}{8}$
$-\frac{1}{2}$

Solve. Check that your answer is reasonable. (5G)

17. Seiji and three of his friends want to share **5** apples. If they share the apples equally, what portion will each person get?

_____

18. A square tile is divided into **4** rectangles. Each rectangle is $\frac{1}{4}$ of the square. What could the tile look like?

_____

Complete each list of multiples. Circle the common multiples. (5A)

1. Multiples of **5**: **10, 15,** _____, _____, _____, _____, _____, **45,** _____

Multiples of **4**: **12,** _____, _____, **24,** _____, _____, _____, _____, **44**

Write an equivalent fraction in simplest form. (5B)

2. $\frac{8}{12}$ _____   **3.** $\frac{9}{15}$ _____

Compare. Write <, >, or =. (5C)

4. $\frac{5}{8}$ ◯ $\frac{2}{3}$ **5.** $\frac{7}{10}$ ◯ $\frac{1}{2}$

Order from least to greatest. (5C)

6. $\frac{5}{8}$ $\frac{1}{4}$ $\frac{1}{2}$ $\frac{2}{3}$ _____

Write each as a fraction. (5D)

7. 5 _____   **8.** $2\frac{4}{5}$ _____

Add or subtract. Write your answer in simplest form. (5E, 5F)

9. $\frac{4}{7}$ $-\frac{2}{7}$

10. $\frac{5}{9}$ $+\frac{7}{9}$

11. $1\frac{2}{5}$ $+1\frac{2}{5}$

12. $3\frac{3}{4}$ $-1\frac{1}{4}$

13. $\frac{2}{8}$ $+\frac{1}{2}$

14. $\frac{1}{3}$ $+\frac{5}{6}$

15. $\frac{5}{8}$ $-\frac{1}{2}$

16. $\frac{5}{6}$ $-\frac{2}{3}$

Solve. Check that your answer is reasonable. (5G)

17. Dean has **5** muffins. If he and two of his friends share the muffins equally, what portion will each person get?

_____

18. A square tile is divided into **4** triangles. Each triangle is $\frac{1}{4}$ of the square. What could the tile look like?

_____

Name the figure. (6A)

1.

_____

2.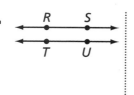

_____

3.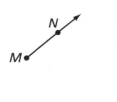

_____

4.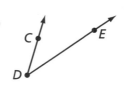

_____

Which figures are congruent? (6B)

 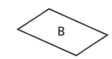

5. _____ and _____

6. _____ and _____

Tell if the angle is *right*, *acute*, or *obtuse*. (6D)

7.

_____

8.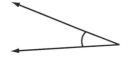

_____

9.

_____

Use the circle to solve. (6F)

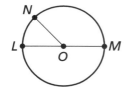

10. Name a radius. _____

11. Name the diameter. _____

Name the kind of turn and its measure in degrees. (6C)

12.

turn _____

degrees _____

13.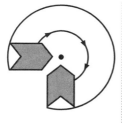

turn _____

degrees _____

14.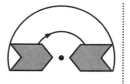

turn _____

degrees _____

15.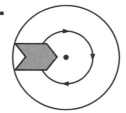

turn _____

degrees _____

Name the figure. (6E, 6G)

16.

_____

17.

_____

18.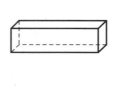

_____

19.

_____

Is the dashed line on the figure a line of symmetry for the figure? Circle _Yes_ or _No._ (6B)

20.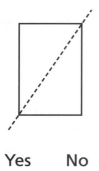

Yes   No

21.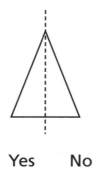

Yes   No

22.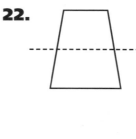

Yes   No

23.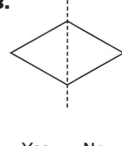

Yes   No

Complete the net for the figure. (6G)

24.

Use the graph to solve. (6H)

25. Which orange juice did about $\frac{1}{2}$ of the people prefer? _____

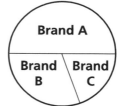

Orange Juice Survey Results

Use the Act It Out Strategy to solve the problem. (6E, 6H)

26. How many quadrilaterals can you make with these two congruent triangles? Name them.

_____

_____

Name the figure. (6A)

1.

_____

2.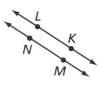

_____

3.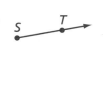

_____

4.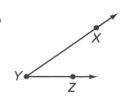

_____

Which figures are congruent? (6B)

     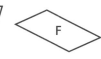

5. _____ and _____

6. _____ and _____

Tell if the angle is *right*, *acute*, or *obtuse*. (6D)

7.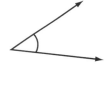

_____

8.

_____

9.

_____

Use the circle to solve. (6F)

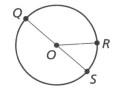

10. Name a radius. _____

11. Name the diameter. _____

Name the kind of turn and its measure in degrees. (6C)

12.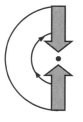

turn _____

degrees _____

13.

turn _____

degrees _____

14.

turn _____

degrees _____

15.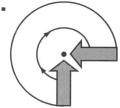

turn _____

degrees _____

Name the figure. (6E, 6G)

16.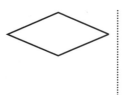

_____

17.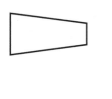

_____

18.

_____

19.

_____

Is the dashed line on the figure a line of symmetry for the figure? Circle *Yes* or *No*. (6B)

20.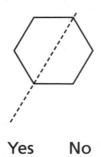

Yes   No

21.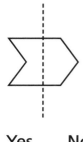

Yes   No

22.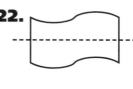

Yes   No

23.

Yes   No

Complete the net for the figure. (6G)

24.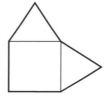

Use the graph to solve. (6H)

25. Which color did about $\frac{1}{2}$ of the people vote for?

_____

Favorite Color

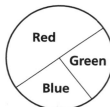

Use the Act It Out Strategy to solve the problem. (6E, 6H)

26. How many triangles can you make with these two congruent triangles? Describe them.

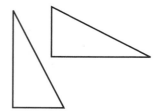

_____

_____

Use a ruler to measure the length of this segment to the nearest inch and to the nearest half inch. (7A)

1. ├──────────────────────────────────┤

_____   _____

Use a ruler to measure the length of this segment to the nearest centimeter and to the nearest millimeter. (7A)

2. ├─────────────────────────┤

_____   _____

Circle the better estimate. (7B)

3. capacity of a bucket

2 gal   **2** pt

4. capacity of a teapot

1 L   **1** mL

5. weight of a boot

1 lb   **1** oz

6. mass of **5** bananas

1 kg   **1** g

Name the equivalent measure. (7C)

7. 2 gal = _____ qt

8. 3 lb = _____ oz

9. 5 yd = _____ ft

10. 16 pt = _____ gal

11. 3 T = _____ lb

12. 5,280 ft = _____ mi

13. 7 cm = _____ mm

14. 8 kg = _____ g

15. 2,000 mL = _____ L

16. 9 ft = _____ yd

17. 5 L = _____ mL

18. 4,000 m = _____ km

Write the letter that indicates the temperature. (7D)

19. 7° C _____

20. ⁻3° C _____

21. 5° F _____

22. ⁻5° F _____

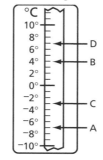

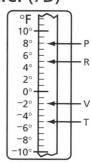

Find the perimeter and area of the figure. (7E, 7F)

23. Perimeter = _____ units

24. Area = _____ square units

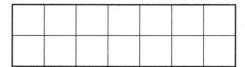

25. Perimeter = _____ cm

26. Area = _____ square cm

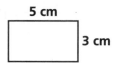

27. Perimeter = _____ units

28. Area = _____ square units

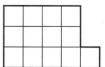

Find the surface area and volume of each rectangular prism. (7G)

29. Surface area = _____ square units

30. Volume = _____ cubic units

31. Surface area = _____ square m

32. Volume = _____ cubic m

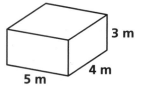

Solve. (7H)

33. Which two letters on this number line are **7** units apart?

_____

34. The two acts of a play are each **30** minutes long. There is a **15**-minute intermission. The play starts at **8:30** P.M. What time does it end? _____

Use a ruler to measure the length of this segment to the nearest inch and to the nearest half inch. (7A)

1. ├─────────────────────────────────┤

_____   _____

Use a ruler to measure the length of this segment to the nearest centimeter and to the nearest millimeter. (7A)

2. ├─────────────────────────────┤

_____   _____

Circle the better estimate. (7B)

3. capacity of a thermos

2 gal   **2 qt**

4. capacity of a watering can

5 L   **5 mL**

5. weight of a pair of glasses

1 lb   **1 oz**

6. mass of **3** potatoes

1 kg   **1 g**

Name the equivalent measure. (7C)

7. 6 yd = _____ ft

8. 9 L = _____ mL

9. 2,000 m = _____ km

10. 8 pt = _____ gal

11. 6 T = _____ lb

12. 2 mi = _____ ft

13. 5 gal = _____ qt

14. 5 lb = _____ oz

15. 15 ft = _____ yd

16. 9 cm = _____ mm

17. 4 kg = _____ g

18. 3,000 mL = _____ L

Write the letter that indicates the temperature. (7D)

19. 8° C _____

20. ⁻4° C _____

21. 6° F _____

22. ⁻6° F _____

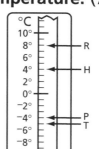
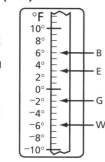

Find the perimeter and area of the figure. (7E, 7F)

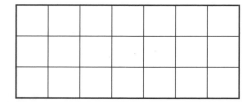

23. Perimeter = _____ units

24. Area = _____ square units

25. Perimeter = _____ cm

26. Area = _____ square cm

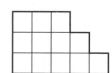

2 cm | 8 cm

27. Perimeter = _____ units

28. Area = _____ square units

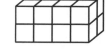

Find the surface area and volume of each rectangular prism. (7G)

29. Surface area = _____ square units

30. Volume = _____ cubic units

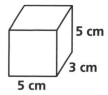

31. Surface area = _____ square m

32. Volume = _____ cubic m

5 cm
3 cm
5 cm

Solve. (7H)

33. Which two letters on this number line are **5** units apart?

_____

A   E   N J   C
0 1 2 3 4 5 6 7 8 9 10

34. The two halves of a concert are each **45** minutes long. There is a **30**-minute intermission. The concert starts at **8:00** P.M. What time does it end? _____

Write the decimal in words. (8A)

1. 3.09 _____   **2.** 0.6 _____

Write the fraction or mixed number as a decimal. (8B)

3. $\frac{2}{5}$ _____   **4.** $3\frac{3}{10}$ _____   **5.** $\frac{1}{4}$ _____   **6.** $5\frac{1}{2}$ _____

Write the decimal as a fraction or mixed number. (8B)

7. 0.7 _____   **8.** 9.07 _____   **9.** 5.9 _____

Compare. Write >, <, or = . (8C)

10. 0.08 ◯ 0.33   **11.** 8.50 ◯ 8.5   **12.** 6.7 ◯ 6.65

Write the decimals in order from greatest to least. (8C)

13. 0.7, 1.4, 2.15, 0.2, 2.55 _____

Round the decimal to the nearest tenth. (8D)

14. 5.24 _____   **15.** 1.75 _____   **16.** 12.88 _____   **17.** 18.47 _____

Round the decimal to the nearest whole number. (8D)

18. 7.63 _____   **19.** 2.49 _____   **20.** 16.37 _____   **21.** 14.81 _____

Find the sum or difference. (8E)

22. 7.6
     + 12.03

23. 5.85
     − 2.44

24. 6.09
     + 8.4

25. 8.2
     − 2.16

Solve. Which number comes next in the sequence? (8F)

26. 0.55, 0.5, 0.45, 0.4, 0.35, 0.3 _____

Cross out the extra information. Then solve the problem. (8F)

27. In a group of **15** hikers, **8** girls and **4** boys are bird watchers. How many hikers are bird watchers? _____

Write the decimal in words. (8A)

1. 7.05 _____

2. 0.9 _____

Write the fraction or mixed number as a decimal. (8B)

3. $\frac{9}{10}$ _____

4. $7\frac{3}{5}$ _____

5. $\frac{1}{4}$ _____

6. $4\frac{3}{4}$ _____

Write the decimal as a fraction or mixed number. (8B)

7. 0.9 _____

8. 14.07 _____

9. 2.1 _____

Compare. Write >, <, or = . (8C)

10. 0.07 ◯ 0.7

11. 4.4 ◯ 4.5

12. 3.8 ◯ 3.80

Write the decimals in order from greatest to least. (8C)

13. 0.3, 2.1, 1.25, 0.5, 2.15 _____

Round the decimal to the nearest tenth. (8D)

14. 7.41 _____

15. 4.36 _____

16. 11.78 _____

17. 12.22 _____

Round the decimal to the nearest whole number. (8D)

18. 2.71 _____

19. 8.28 _____

20. 12.51 _____

21. 18.36 _____

Find the sum or difference. (8E)

22. $\begin{array}{r} 3.7 \\ + 16.02 \\ \hline \end{array}$

23. $\begin{array}{r} 9.65 \\ - 7.23 \\ \hline \end{array}$

24. $\begin{array}{r} 5.04 \\ + 5.2 \\ \hline \end{array}$

25. $\begin{array}{r} 8.8 \\ - 6.62 \\ \hline \end{array}$

Solve. Which number comes next in the sequence? (8F)

26. 0.5, 0.75, 1, 1.25, 1.5, 1.75 _____

Cross out the extra information. Then solve the problem. (8F)

27. In a group of **28** campers, **14** girls and **11** boys like to play volleyball. How many campers like to play volleyball?

_____

Divide. (9A, 9B)

1. $14\overline{)84}$

2. $38\overline{)51}$

3. $42\overline{)315}$

4. $19\overline{)570}$

5. $27\overline{)2,466}$

6. $44\overline{)9,352}$

7. $32\overline{)6,656}$

8. $17\overline{)6,975}$

9. $41\overline{)5,163}$

Write compatible numbers you could use to estimate the quotient. Then write the estimate. (9C)

10. $62\overline{)371}$

    Compatible numbers

    _____

    Estimate _____

11. $25\overline{)7,410}$

    Compatible numbers

    _____

    Estimate _____

Solve. (9D)

12. For their **10th** anniversary, Just Toys gave every **5th** customer a balloon and every **20th** customer a stuffed animal. Just Toys had **360** visitors on their anniversary. How many balloons and how many stuffed animals were given away?

_____

13. Mark cut a rope into **3** equal lengths. He then cut each of the 3 pieces into **5** equal lengths. How many pieces of rope does he have now?

_____

Divide. (9A, 9B)

1. $16\overline{)96}$

2. $58\overline{)77}$

3. $86\overline{)442}$

4. $14\overline{)560}$

5. $28\overline{)1,376}$

6. $42\overline{)8,723}$

7. $31\overline{)9,486}$

8. $12\overline{)5,422}$

9. $19\overline{)3,158}$

Write compatible numbers you could use to estimate the quotient. Then write the estimate. (9C)

10. $71\overline{)287}$

Compatible numbers

_____

Estimate _____

11. $25\overline{)5,110}$

Compatible numbers

_____

Estimate _____

Solve. (9D)

12. Yolanda waters her plants every **6** days. She mows her lawn every **10** days. In **120** days, how many times does Yolanda water her plants? How many times does she mow her lawn?

_____

13. Jason is building a fence around a **12**-foot by **18**-foot rectangular garden. If he puts a fence post every **6** feet, how many fence posts does he need?

_____

Arrange the data in order from least to greatest.
Then find the range, median, mode, and outlier. (10B)

1. 41, 44, 92, 27, 41, 39, 29, 30 _____

   range: _____   median: _____   mode: _____   outlier: _____

2. 63, 72, 12, 68, 74, 70, 68, 75 _____

   range: _____   median: _____   mode: _____   outlier: _____

Use the table to make a line graph
on the grid below. (10A)

3. Use a scale of **0, 5, 10, 15, 20, 25, 30** to complete the vertical axis.

4. Complete the horizontal axis by writing the name of each month.

5. Graph the weight of the puppy for each month. Connect the points with line segments.

6. In what month did the puppy weigh **22** pounds?

   _____

7. Describe how the puppy's weight changed between April and May.

   _____

   _____

Puppy's Growth	
Month	Weight (lb)
March	3
April	9
May	14
June	18
July	22
August	28

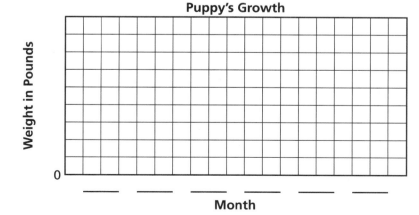

Puppy's Growth

Weight in Pounds

0

Month

Use the spinner to answer each question. (10C, 10D)

8. What is the chance that the spinner will point to a star?

_____

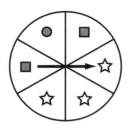

9. Which outcome is more likely to occur: the spinner pointing to a circle or the spinner pointing to a square?

_____

Complete the tree diagram to show all of the possible outfits. The pants are jeans. The shirts are red, blue, or yellow. The shoes are black or brown. (10C)

10. Pants   Shirts   Shoes

Jeans

11. How many different possible outfits are there? _____

Make a shopping list showing the total amount of each ingredient needed to make these two recipes. Then answer the question. (10F)

12. Shopping List

_____

_____

_____

_____

Berry Dessert	Cool Drink
3 pt strawberries	1 qt cranberry juice
$1\frac{1}{2}$ c blackberries	$1\frac{1}{2}$ pt strawberries
$1\frac{1}{2}$ pt blueberries	$1\frac{1}{2}$ pt blueberries
2 qt vanilla yogurt	$\frac{3}{4}$ c blackberries

13. Which ingredient do you need the greatest amount of?

How much do you need? _____

_____

Arrange the data in order from least to greatest.
Then find the range, median, mode, and outlier. (10B)

1. **26, 36, 29, 35, 31, 26, 84, 40** _____

range: _____   median: _____   mode: _____   outlier: _____

2. **52, 5, 48, 50, 61, 64, 56, 60** _____

range: _____   median: _____   mode: _____   outlier: _____

Use the table to make a line graph
on the grid below. (10A)

3. Use a scale of **0, 10, 20, 30, 40, 50, 60** to complete
the vertical axis.

4. Complete the horizontal axis by writing the
number of each week.

5. Graph the running time for each week. Connect
the points with line segments.

6. Between what two weeks did the running time
decrease the most?

_____

7. Describe how the running time changed between
week **4** and week **5**.

_____

_____

Skill Growth	
Week	Running Time (sec)
1	55
2	45
3	38
4	33
5	29
6	27

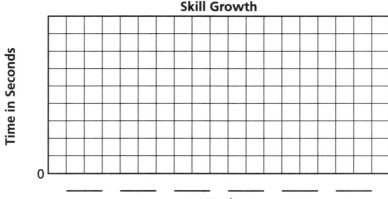

Skill Growth

Time in Seconds

0

Week

Use the spinner to answer each question. (10C, 10D)

8. What is the chance that the spinner will point to a circle?

_____

9. Which outcome is more likely to occur: the spinner pointing to a star or the spinner pointing to a square?

_____

Make a tree diagram to show all of the possible lunches. The sandwich is peanut butter. The salad is potato, green, or fruit. The soup is bean or carrot. (10E)

10. Sandwich   Salad   Soup

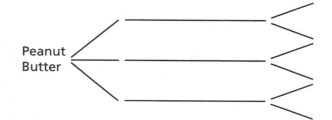

Peanut Butter

11. How many different possible lunches are there? _____

Make a shopping list showing the total amount of each ingredient needed to make these two recipes. Then answer the question. (10F)

Mango Drink	Party Fruit Punch
3 qt tangerine juice	$2\frac{1}{2}$ c pineapple
$1\frac{1}{2}$ pt strawberries	$5\frac{1}{2}$ pt strawberries
$1\frac{1}{2}$ pt mango juice	$3\frac{1}{2}$ qt tangerine juice
$\frac{3}{4}$ c pineapple	2 pt blackberries

12. Shopping List

_____

_____

_____

_____

13. Which ingredient do you need the greatest amount of?

How much do you need? _____

_____

Choose a variable for the unknown number.
Then write an algebraic expression for the word phrase. (11A)

Word Phrase	Variable	Algebraic Expression
1. 3 less than a number	_____	_____
2. a number divided by **4**	_____	_____
3. three times a length	_____	_____

Circle the value for the variable that makes
the equation balanced. (11C)

4. $14 - w = 8$ 5   6   7   **5.** $x + 24 = 54$ 20   30   78

6. $5 \times m = 40$ 5   8   10   **7.** $23 - c = 8$ 35   25   15

Solve the equation. (11C)

8. $t \times 6 = 42$ $t =$ _____   **9.** $y + 12 = 47$ $y =$ _____

10. $5 \times n = 35$ $n =$ _____   **11.** $13 + r = 50$ $r =$ _____

Write an algebraic equation for the word sentence.
Then find the solution. Use _n_ for the variable. (11A, 11B)

12. Three more than some number is **12**. What is the number?

_____ $n =$ _____

13. The sum of Troy's age and **14** is **30**. What is Troy's age?

_____ $n =$ _____

14. A number divided by **8** is **3**. What is the number?

_____ $n =$ _____

15. The difference between some number and _n_ is **13**.
What is the number?

_____ $n =$ _____

Write an algebraic equation for each word sentence. Then find the solution. Use *n* for the variable. (11A, 11B)

16. The number of muffins baked less the **6** that were eaten is **12**. What is the number of muffins baked?

_____   *n* = _____

17. Double the frame's height is **24** inches. What is the frame's height?

_____   *n* = _____

Complete the function table for the rule and the values of *x* listed. Write and graph the ordered pairs. (11D)

$y = x - 2$

x	*x* − 2	*y*
6	6 − 2	4
5		
4		
3		

18. (row with 5)
19. (row with 4)
20. (row with 3)

Ordered Pairs

(6,4)

_____

_____

_____

21. If you connected the points on the graph, what would you draw? _____

Solve. (11E)

22. Brad has **14** shells. That is **6** more shells than his brother Wayne has. What number sentence could be used to find the number of shells Wayne has? How many shells does Wayne have?

_____

Cross out the extra information. Then solve the problem. (11E)

23. Paula bought some clay for **$12.56** and a modeling tool for **$5.79**. She gave the clerk **$20**. How much did Paula spend on art supplies?

_____

**Choose a variable for the unknown number.
Then write an algebraic expression for the word phrase.** (11A)

Word Phrase	Variable	Algebraic Expression
1. 8 less than a number	_____	_____
2. the product of **5** and a number	_____	_____
3. three times a length	_____	_____

**Circle the value for the variable that makes
the equation balanced.** (11C)

4. $16 - p = 8$ 6   7   8

5. $k + 17 = 37$ 20   30   54

6. $9 \times f = 72$ 8   9   10

7. $18 - n = 9$ 27   18   9

Solve the equation. (11C)

8. $m \times 4 = 28$ $m =$ _____

9. $r + 13 = 52$ $r =$ _____

10. $8 \times y = 72$ $y =$ _____

11. $25 + n = 30$ $n =$ _____

**Write an algebraic equation for the word sentence.
Then find the solution. Use *n* for the variable.** (11A, 11B)

12. Seven less than some number is **5**. What is the number?

_____ $n =$ _____

13. The sum of Jack's height and **12** inches is **75** inches. How tall is Jack?

_____ $n =$ _____

14. A number times **7** is **56**. What is the number?

_____ $n =$ _____

15. A number divided by **9** is **7**. What is the number?

_____ $n =$ _____

Write an algebraic equation for each word sentence. Then find the solution. Use *n* for the variable. (11A, 11B)

16. The number of eggs less the **6** cracked eggs is **20**. What is the number of eggs?

_____   *n* = _____

17. The pumpkin's weight tripled is **75** pounds. How much does the pumpkin weigh?

_____   *n* = _____

Complete the function table for the rule and the values of *x* listed. Write and graph the ordered pairs. (11D)

$y = x + 2$ Ordered Pairs

x	*x* + 2	*y*
0	0 + 2	2
1		
3		
4		

(0,2)

_____

_____

_____

18.
19.
20.

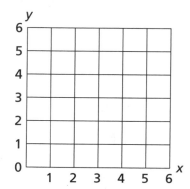

21. If you connect the points on the graph, what will you draw? _____

Solve. (11E)

22. The length of a rectangle is **5** inches greater than its width. The rectangle's length is **17** inches.

What is its width? _____

Cross out the extra information. Then solve the problem. (11E)

23. Tickets to a concert cost **$35**. The number of tickets sold is **1,212**, and there are **1,008** tickets left. How many concert tickets are there in all?

_____

1 Which is the standard form for two thousand, nine hundred seven?

A 29,707

B 2,907

C 297

D 207

2 Grant sold 145 raffle tickets. Linda sold 10 fewer tickets than Grant. Gail sold 20 more tickets than Linda. How many raffle tickets did Gail sell?

F 245   H 135

G 155   J 100

3 On Thursday, thirty-four thousand, three hundred fifty-six copies of the Daily News were printed. Which shows this number in standard form?

A 34,000,356

B 3,403,056

C 340,356

D 34,356

4 A garden has 4 congruent sides and 4 right angles. Which is the shape of the garden?

F square

G rectangle

H trapezoid

J parallelogram

5 If the pattern continues, how many birdhouses will Andrea make next week?

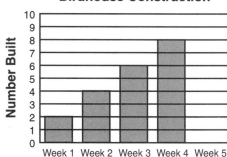

Birdhouse Construction

8   10   12   14
A   B   C   D

6 Rose found 735 + 219 = 954. Which expression can she use to check her addition?

F 954 − 219

G 954 + 219

H 735 − 954

J 735 − 219

7 Which number makes this number sentence true?

$5 + 6 = 6 + \boxed{}$

A 1   C 6

B 5   D 11

8 What is the value of this expression?

$(6 + 2) \times 4$

F 12   H 32

G 16   J 48

9 Which expression is equal to $(5 \times 6) \times 3$?

A $5 \times (6 \times 3)$ C 11×3

B $(5 + 6) + 3$ D $5 \times (6 \div 3)$

10 Which are the factors of 18?

F 1, 2, 3, 6, 9, 18

G 1, 2, 4, 8, 12, 18

H 1, 3, 4, 6, 9, 18

J 1, 2, 5, 15, 18

11 Which number is divisible by both 3 and 5?

A 9   C 12

B 10   D 15

12 How many more flowers did Colin plant than Becky?

Flowers Planted

Colin   ✿ ✿ ✿ ✿ ✿
Becky   ✿ ✿ ✿
Serge   ✿ ✿ ✿ ✿

Key ✿ = 4 flowers

F 12   H 8

G 10   J 6

13 Bob got $6.25 in change when he bought 3 pens that cost $1.25 each. How much money did Bob pay?

A $3.75   C $8.50

B $7.75   D $10.00

14 Which is $\frac{12}{18}$ in simplest form?

F $\frac{6}{9}$ H $\frac{3}{4}$

G $\frac{4}{5}$ J $\frac{2}{3}$

15 Which is a multiple of both 4 and 6?

A 2   C 12

B 10   D 15

16 Antonio needs 14 batteries. There are 4 batteries in a package. How many packages should he buy?

F 3   H 8

G 4   J 14

17 Who has woven the greatest fraction of a rug?

Rug Weaving	
Name	Part Woven
Sharon	$\frac{1}{3}$
Thomas	$\frac{3}{5}$
Anne	$\frac{1}{2}$
Roland	$\frac{3}{8}$

A Sharon   C Anne

B Thomas   D Roland

18 Which mixed number is equal to $\frac{11}{4}$?

F $1\frac{1}{4}$ H $2\frac{3}{4}$

G $2\frac{1}{4}$ J $3\frac{3}{4}$

19 Mason rotated his house plant one half turn. How many degrees did he rotate the plant?

A 90°

B 180°

C 270°

D 360°

20 Which two streets are parallel?

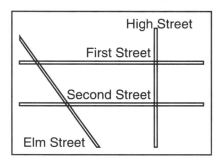

F High and First

G First and Second

H Second and High

J Elm and First

21 Which two shapes are congruent?

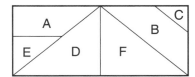

A C and E

B A and B

C D and F

D E and D

22 Chinua bought a baseball cap for $6.89. He gave the clerk $10. Which shows his change?

F

G

H

J

23 If you cut out and fold this pattern, which geometric solid will you make?

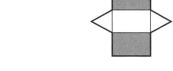

A   **C**

B   **D**

24 Who sold about $\frac{2}{5}$ of the cards?

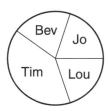

F Bev   **H** Lou

G Jo   **J** Tim

25   456
        + 332

A 766   D 788

B 776   E 789

C 786

26   2,876
        + 23,788

F 2,329   J 4,329

G 3,229   K NH

H 4,229

27   54,271
        + 23,788

A 30,483   D 77,969

B 77,059   E 78,059

C 77,959

28   694
        − 367

F 223   J 333

G 237   K NH

H 327

29   39,108
        − 5,712

A 23,216   D 34,496

B 33,396   E 44,820

C 33,496

30   356
           24
        + 474

F 732   J 832

G 734   K 854

H 754

31   45
        × 4

A 165   D 810

B 180   E NH

C 216

32   306
        × 7

F 63   J 2,142

G 252   K 2,242

H 2,135

33 67
$\times$ 42

A 382   **C** 2,504   **E** NH

B 402   **D** 2,714

34 314
$\times$ 52

F 2,198   **J** 16,328

G 15,128   **K** 17,328

H 16,128

35 5)‾79‾

A 11 R4   **C** 15 R4   **E** NH

B 15   **D** 16 R1

36 6)‾252‾

F 39   **H** 43   **K** 44

G 42   **J** 43 R2

37 3)‾1,563‾

A 497   **C** 521   **E** NH

B 509   **D** 561

38 $\dfrac{3}{7}$
$+\dfrac{2}{7}$

F $\dfrac{1}{7}$ **H** $\dfrac{5}{21}$ **K** 1

G $\dfrac{5}{14}$ **J** $\dfrac{5}{7}$

39 $\dfrac{7}{8}$
$-\dfrac{5}{8}$

A $\dfrac{1}{8}$ **C** $\dfrac{3}{8}$ **E** NH

B $\dfrac{1}{4}$ **D** $\dfrac{1}{2}$

40 $4\dfrac{5}{6}$
$-2\dfrac{1}{6}$

F $1\dfrac{2}{3}$ **H** $2\dfrac{1}{5}$ **K** $2\dfrac{2}{3}$

G $2\dfrac{1}{6}$ **J** $2\dfrac{1}{2}$

41 $\dfrac{1}{2}$
$-\dfrac{3}{8}$

A $\dfrac{1}{8}$ **C** $\dfrac{1}{4}$ **E** NH

B $\dfrac{3}{16}$ **D** $\dfrac{5}{8}$

42 $\dfrac{1}{3}$
$+\dfrac{1}{4}$

F $\dfrac{1}{12}$ **H** $\dfrac{2}{7}$ **K** $\dfrac{3}{4}$

G $\dfrac{1}{7}$ **J** $\dfrac{7}{12}$

43 Patty bought a muffin for $1.25 and a carton of milk for $.69. She gave the clerk $5. How much change should she get back?

A $3.06   D $1.94

B $2.96   E NH

C $2.06

44 Vivian pays $420 for rent each month. How much rent does she pay in 3 months?

F $126   J $840

G $140   K $1,260

H $423

45 About how many people attended the play on these three nights?

Play Attendance	
Friday	315
Saturday	297
Sunday	288

A 800   D 1,200

B 900   E NH

C 1,000

46 Marsha ate $\frac{3}{10}$ of the pizza. Miguel ate $\frac{4}{10}$ of the pizza. What fraction of the pizza did they eat altogether?

F $\frac{1}{10}$ H $\frac{3}{5}$ K $\frac{4}{5}$

G $\frac{7}{20}$ J $\frac{7}{10}$

47 If a heart beats 70 times each minute, how many times does it beat in 10 minutes?

A 700

B 7,000

C 70,000

D 700,000

E NH

48 What is the average cost of a stamp?

F 14¢

G 17¢

H 19¢

J 23¢

K 68¢

49 Postcards are priced at 4 for $1.20. What is the cost of one postcard?

A $.40   D $.25

B $.35   E NH

C $.30

50 Which of the numbers shows 473,265 rounded to the nearest thousand?

F 500,000   J 400,000

G 470,000   K 47,000

H 473,000

Assessments

1 Which decimal shows where the arrow is pointing on the ruler?

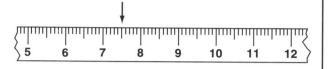

A 7 cm

B 7.5 cm

C 8 cm

D 0.75 cm

2 How many 10-centimeter blocks can be cut from a board 83 cm long?

F 3

G 8

H 10

J 18

3 Use your centimeter ruler to help you answer this question. How long is the toothpick?

A 2 cm

B 5 cm

C 7 cm

D 9 cm

4 Which is the best estimate of the capacity of a soda bottle?

F 2 mL

G 20 mL

H 2 L

J 20 L

5 Which is the best estimate of the weight of a one-week-old puppy?

A 4 oz

B 4 lb

C 40 lb

D 4 T

6 If Margie were 5 inches taller, her height would be 62 inches. Which number sentence could you use to find Margie's height?

F $m + 5 = 62$

G $m = 62 + 5$

H $5 - m = 62$

J $62 \times 5 = m$

7 Which number makes the equation true?

$$(3 + 5) \times 7 = 8 \times \boxed{}$$

A 56

B 15

C 8

D 7

8 Which is the rule for this function table?

x	y
3	6
4	8
5	10
6	12

F $y = x + 3$

G $y = 3x$

H $y = \frac{1}{2}x$

J $y = 2x$

9 What are the coordinates of point A?

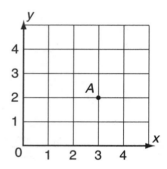

A (2,2) **C** (3,2)

B (2,3) **D** (3,3)

10 Isabel bought 5 cartons of cat food. Each carton contains 24 cans. If each of her 3 cats eats 2 cans of cat food a day, how many days will the cat food last?

F 60

G 40

H 30

J 20

11 If you draw one of the cards without looking, what is the probability that you will draw an X?

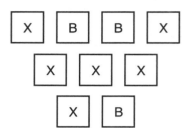

A $\frac{6}{3}$ **C** $\frac{1}{2}$

B $\frac{2}{3}$ **D** $\frac{3}{5}$

12 Suppose you have a blue shirt, a green shirt, and a white shirt. You also have a red sweater and a black sweater. How many sweater and shirt combinations can you make?

F 4 **H** 6

G 5 **J** 12

13 What is the difference between today's high and low temperatures?

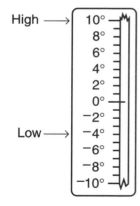

A 8° **C** 12°

B 10° **D** 14°

14 Tracy bought 2 yards of ribbon. How many inches of ribbon is that?

F 18 in.

G 24 in.

H 48 in.

J 72 in.

15 What is the volume of a box that is 18 inches wide, 24 inches long, and 12 inches tall?

A 54 cubic inches

B 432 cubic inches

C 3,458 cubic inches

D 5,184 cubic inches

16 Which is the decimal for sixty-three hundredths?

F 6.3

G 6.03

H 0.63

J 0.063

17 John wants $\frac{3}{4}$ pound of cheese. Which package should he buy?

A 0.34 lb

B 3.4 1b

C 0.5 lb

D 0.75 lb

18 Which of the trails is the longest?

East Trail	10.4 km
West Trail	10.67 km
South Trail	10.49 km
North Trail	10.6 km

F East Trail

G West Trail

H South Trail

J North Trail

19 The graph shows the cost of building various numbers of toy wagons. Predict the cost of building 3 wagons.

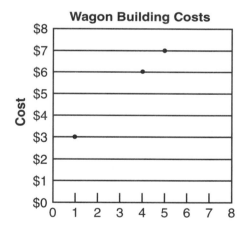

A $5

B $6

C $8

D $10

20 The line plot shows the ages of the members of the middle school student council. How many student council members are there?

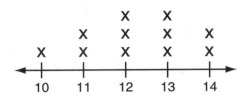

F 11

G 12

H 13

J 14

21 What is the length of the perimeter of a rectangular house that is 42 feet long and 34 feet wide?

A 1,426 ft

B 304 ft

C 152 ft

D 76 ft

22 Which is 5,000,000 + 30,000 + 800 in standard form?

F 5,380,000

G 5,030,800

H 5,003,800

J 5,000,380

23 This drawing shows the foundation of a house. What is the area of the house?

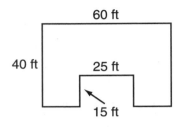

A 2,775 square feet

B 2,400 square feet

C 2,025 square feet

D 1,775 square feet

24 Which is the diameter of this circle?

F $\overline{RS}$ **H** $\overline{RT}$

G $\overline{VR}$ **J** $\overline{TV}$

25 Which describes angle *M*?

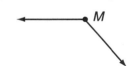

A acute

B right

C obtuse

D congruent

Assessments

Use the graph for problems 26 and 27.

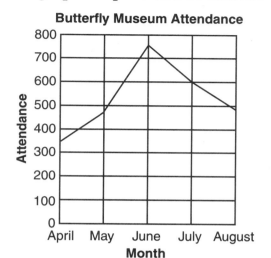

Butterfly Museum Attendance

26 In which month did the greatest number of people go to the butterfly museum?

F May

G June

H July

J August

27 In which two months was attendance about the same?

A April and June

B May and August

C July and August

D April and July

28 Which of these numbers is prime?

F 21

G 27

H 34

J 37

29 What is the value of these bills and coins?

A $3.36

B $3.90

C $2.65

D $2.05

30 What is the value of this expression?

$$8 \div 2 + 2$$

F 2   H 6

G 4   J 12

31 Leslie performed this experiment: Draw a marble out of the bag. Tally the result. Put the marble back in the bag.

	Tally	Total
Blue	III	3
Green	||||| II	7
Red	||||| ||||| II	12
Black	III	3

Which color marble do you predict there were the most of in the bag?

A blue

B green

C red

D black

32   2.4
        + 3.7

F 1.3   J 6.3

G 5.3   K NH

H 5.7

33   8.6
        − 5.9

A 3.7   D 2.3

B 3.3   E 1.7

C 2.7

34   4.65
        + 6.09

F 10.54

G 10.64

H 10.74

J 11.64

K 11.74

35   28.04
        − 5.71

A 21.23

B 22.33

C 22.75

D 32.75

E NH

36 $24\overline{)76}$

F 2 R8

G 3 R1

H 3 R4

J 4 R2

K 4 R3

37 $39\overline{)95}$

A 5

B 6

C 7

D 8

E NH

38 $16\overline{)2,592}$

F 162

G 182

H 882

J 1,620

K 1,682

In her past seven basketball games, Ellen scored 10, 15, 14, 10, 12, 13, and 10 points.

39 What is the range for the number of points Ellen scored?

A 15   D 5

B 12   E NH

C 7

40 What is the median number of points Ellen scored?

F 10   J 13

G 11   K 14

H 12

41 What is the mode number of points Ellen scored?

A 10   D 15

B 12   E NH

C 14

42 What is the mean number of points Ellen scored?

F 10   J 13

G 11   K 14

H 12

43 Each of the 492 students taking a test needs a pencil. Pencils come in boxes of 25. How many boxes are needed?

A 25   D 19

B 21   E NH

C 20

44 Which of these numbers shows 8.73 rounded to the nearest tenth?

F 9   J 8.3

G 8.8   K 8

H 8.7

45 Last week George earned $245. This week he earned $315. How much did he earn in the two weeks?

A $450

B $550

C $560

D $660

E NH

46 Carmela drives 24 miles each day. How far does she drive in 5 days?

F 12 miles

G 100 miles

H 120 miles

J 130 miles

K 140 miles

47 Sofia practices the tuba for 25 minutes each day. How many minutes did she practice in January? (Remember that January has 31 days.)

A 100 minutes

B 635 minutes

C 775 minutes

D 7,525 minutes

E NH

48 Enrique bought a shirt for $25.96 and a belt for $28.69. How much did he spend?

F $43.55

G $44.65

H $53.65

J $54.55

K $54.65

49 Tina made 360 jars of jam. She is putting the jars in cases of 12 jars each. How many cases does she need?

A 30

B 36

C 44

D 42

E NH

50 Greg borrowed $1,320 from his father. He is going to pay it back in 24 equal payments. How much will each payment be?

F $64

G $56

H $55

J $45

K $40

51 Randy mowed $\frac{2}{5}$ of the lawn. Janice mowed $\frac{1}{2}$ of the lawn. What fractional part more did Janice mow?

A $\frac{1}{10}$

B $\frac{1}{5}$

C $\frac{4}{5}$

D $\frac{9}{10}$

E NH

52 Akira bought 84 miniature cars. The cars come in boxes of 14. How many boxes did he buy?

F 12

G 9

H 7

J 6

K 5

Reteach Worksheets

NOTES

58

● What number is shown with the place-value blocks?

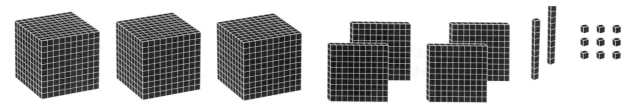

You can use a place-value chart to help you write the number in different ways.

Standard form: 3,429

Expanded form: 3,000 + 400 + 20 + 9
In expanded form, the value of each place is written separately.

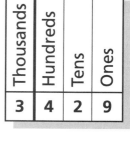

Thousands	Hundreds	Tens	Ones
3	4	2	9

Word form: three thousand, four hundred twenty-nine

If there were no hundreds blocks above, you would write a zero in the hundreds place.

↓
3,029

● **What number is shown? Write the number in three ways.**

1.

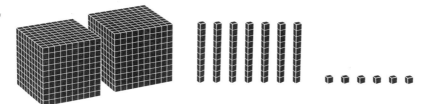

Standard form: _____   Expanded form: _____

Word form: _____

Write the value of the 3 in each number.

2. 135   **3.** 1,387   **4.** 3,564   **5.** 2,386   **6.** 5,003

____   ____   ____   ____   ____

Write the number in standard form and expanded form.

7. fifty-two _____   **8.** eight thousand, seven hundred _____

● **Write the number in word form.**

9. 24 _____   **10.** 726 _____

You can use a place-value chart to show greater numbers. This place-value chart is separated into groups of **3 columns** each. Each group is a period.

The period on the right is the **ones period.**
The period on the left is the **thousands period.**

Here are some ways to write the same number.

Standard form: 32,453

Expanded form: 30,000 + 2,000 + 400 + 50 + 3

Word form: thirty-two thousand, four hundred fifty-three

Thousands Period			Ones Period		
Hundreds	Tens	Ones	Hundreds	Tens	Ones
	3	2	4	5	3

A comma separates the ones period from the thousands period.

Write the number in the place-value chart.

1. 54,382

2. 20,000 + 6,000 + 500 + 2

3. 8,000 + 900 + 70 + 6

4. twelve thousand, ninety

	Thousands Period			Ones Period		
	Hundreds	Tens	Ones	Hundreds	Tens	Ones
1.						
2.						
3.						
4.						

Place the missing comma. Write the number in word form.

5. 4 2 4 3 8 _____

6. 9 3 5 3 _____

7. 2 7 0 0 0 _____

Write the number in expanded form.

8. 25,432

9. 64,890

_____

_____

Teacher Note: Use before Unit 1, Lesson 1. **(4)**

You can use a place-value chart to help you read and write greater numbers.

The place-value chart shows the number **307,215**. The comma separates the thousands and the ones and also makes it easier to read the number.

Thousands			Ones		
Hundreds	Tens	Ones	Hundreds	Tens	Ones
3	0	7	2	1	5

Follow these steps to read **307,215**.

Underline the digits to the left of the comma.

307,215

Read the underlined number and say "thousand."

Read the last part of the number.

307 thousand, 215

or

three hundred seven thousand, two hundred fifteen

Write the number in words.

1.

Thousands			Ones		
Hundreds	Tens	Ones	Hundreds	Tens	Ones
	6	8	0	1	2

sixty-eight _____, twelve

2.

Thousands			Ones		
Hundreds	Tens	Ones	Hundreds	Tens	Ones
5	6	2	1	0	3

_____ thousand _____

3. **16,812** _____

4. **9,100** _____

5. **37,360** _____

6. **183,004** _____

7. **362,540** _____

8. **945,251** _____

Name _____

Which is greater, **132** or **136**?

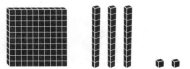 

Start comparing the digits at the left because it is the
place with the greatest value.

Compare hundreds.   →   **1** hundred = **1** hundred

Compare tens.   →   **3** tens = **3** tens

Compare ones.   →   **2** ones < **6** ones

So **132** is less than **136**.

< means "is less than"	> means "is greater than"
132 < 136	**136 > 132**

Compare. Write < or >.

1.

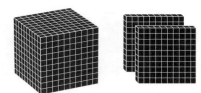

1,210 _____ 1,304

2.

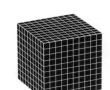

327 _____ 245

---

3. 712 _____ 625   **4.** 1,256 _____ 1,156   **5.** 270 _____ 207

6. 3,255 _____ 6,411   **7.** 5,000 _____ 5,001   **8.** 7,330 _____ 7,303

9. 1,824 _____ 1,819   **10.** 3,842 _____ 3,257   **11.** 4,010 _____ 4,100

Teacher Note: Use after Quick Check page 8 to reteach Unit 1, Lesson 2. **(4)**

Round **1,277** to the nearest thousand.

| Underline the place you are rounding to. **1,2 7 7** | Circle the place to the right of the underlined digit. **1 ②7 7** If the circled digit is **5** or greater, round up. If it is less than **5**, round down. | Round to the nearest thousand. Since **2 < 5**, round down to **1,000**. |

Complete the table to round to the nearest hundred.

	Underline the hundreds place.	Circle the tens place.	Round.
1. 402	402	402	
2. 340	340	340	
3. 280	280	280	

Round to the nearest hundred.

4. 485   **5.** 914   **6.** 857   **7.** 286   **8.** 130

_____   _____   _____   _____   _____

Complete the table to round to the nearest thousand.

	Underline the thousands place.	Circle the hundreds place.	Round.
9. 5,781	5,781	5,781	
10. 3,289	3,289	3,289	
11. 2,043	2,043	2,043	

Round to the nearest ten.

12. 3,572   **13.** 1,203   **14.** 7,248   **15.** 2,510   **16.** 3,751

_____   _____   _____   _____   _____

Teacher Note: Use after Quick Check page 8 to reteach Unit 1, Lesson 3. **(4)**   **63**

You can use the commas in a number written in standard form to help you read and write the number.

| The commas help you see the number of periods. **78,162,800** This number has **3 periods.** | Determine the greatest period. **1 period** → Ones **2 periods** → Thousands **3 periods** → Millions The greatest period is millions. | Write the word name for the number. Then write the period name. For the ones period, write just the word name for the number. "Seventy-eight million, one hundred sixty-two thousand, eight hundred" |

Write the name of the greatest period for each number.

1. 9,235,100	**2.** 292,003	**3.** 8,000,000	**4.** 150
_____	_____	_____	_____
5. 701,953,708	**6.** 325	**7.** 326,472	**8.** 16,439,031
_____	_____	_____	_____

Complete the word name for each number.

9. 6,054,100   six _____, fifty-four _____, one hundred

10. 81,109,000   eighty-one _____, one hundred nine _____

11. 634,004,060   six hundred thirty-four _____, four _____, sixty

Write the word name for each number.

12. 1,563,000   _____

13. 555,000,000   _____

14. 82,700,004   _____

Write the number in standard form.

15. two million, one hundred twenty-one thousand   _____

16. nineteen million, one hundred ninety-four   _____

17. one hundred eight million, forty-five thousand, ten   _____

Teacher Note: Use after Quick Check page 14 to reteach Unit 1, Lesson 5. **(4)**

Round **54,329** to the nearest thousand.

| Underline the place you are rounding to.

5 <u>4</u>, 3 2 9 | Circle the place to the right of the underlined digit.

5 <u>4</u>,③ 2 9

If the circled digit is 5 or greater, round up. If it is less than 5, round down. | Round to the nearest thousand.

54,000

Remember to write zeros in all places to the right of the place you are rounding to. |

Underline the place named and circle the place to the right. Then round to the place named.

1. ten thousands
3,074,184

_____

2. thousands
92,868

_____

3. hundred thousands
1,871,348

_____

4. hundred thousands
2,713,840

_____

5. thousands
354,897

_____

6. ten thousands
871,200

_____

Round each number to the places given.

	hundreds	thousands
7. 10,482,787	_____	_____
8. 3,709,810	_____	_____
9. 253,893,611	_____	_____
10. 512,746,329	_____	_____
11. 59,974,056	_____	_____

Write the place the number has been rounded to.

12. 16,534,876 → 16,500,000 _____

13. 10,693,231 → 10,693,000 _____

14. 21,966,670 → 21,970,000 _____

Teacher Note: Use after Quick Check page 14 to reteach Unit 1, Lesson 6. **(4)**

Commutative Property of Addition

If you change the order of the addends, the sum stays
the same.

▲▲ + ▲▲▲▲▲ = ▲▲▲▲▲▲▲   ▲▲▲▲▲ + ▲▲ = ▲▲▲▲▲▲▲

   2   +   5   =   7 ← sum   5   +   2   =   7 ← sum
   ↑   ↑   ↑   ↑
addend addend   addend   addend

$$2 + 5 = 5 + 2$$

Associative Property of Addition

If you change the way the addends are grouped, the
sum stays the same.

▲▲ + (▲ + ▲▲▲) =   (▲▲ + ▲) + ▲▲▲ =
 2 + (1 + 3) =   (2 + 1) + 3 =

▲▲ + ▲▲▲▲ = ▲▲▲▲▲▲   ▲▲▲ + ▲▲▲ = ▲▲▲▲▲▲
 2 +   4   =   6   3   + 3 = 6

$$2 + (1 + 3) = (2 + 1) + 3$$

Use the Commutative Property of Addition to complete.

1. ● + ●● = ●● + ●
    ●● ●● ●● ●●

    _3_ + _4_ = ____ + ____

2. $5 + 8 = $ _____ $+ 5$

3. $7 + 3 = 3 + $ _____

Use the Associative Property of Addition to complete.

4. $3 + (2 + 4) = ($ ____ $+$ ____ $) + 4$

   $3 + $ ____ $ = $ ____ $+ 4$

   ____ $ = $ ____

....

5. $8 + (2 + 3) = (8 + 2) + 3$

   $8 + $ _____ $ = $ _____ $+ 3$

   _____ $ = $ _____

6. $(4 + 1) + 3 = 4 + (1 + 3)$

   _____ $+ 3 = 4 + $ _____

   _____ $ = $ _____

Teacher Note: Use after Quick Check page 26 to reteach Unit 2, Lesson 1. (4)

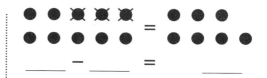

Subtraction and addition are **inverse operations.**

$$4 + 5 = 9 \qquad 9 - 5 = 4$$

Notice that the same numbers are used in both number sentences: **4, 5,** and **9.**

The number sentences $4 + 5 = 9$ and $9 - 5 = 4$ are related.

Complete the related number sentences.

1.

$\underline{\ 7\ } + \underline{\ 3\ } = \underline{\ \ \ \ }$ $\qquad$ $\underline{\ \ \ } - \underline{\ \ \ } = \underline{\ \ \ }$

---

2. $8 + 2 = 10$

$10 - 2 = \underline{\ \ \ \ }$

3. $6 + 5 = 11$

$11 - 5 = \underline{\ \ \ \ }$

4. $9 - 7 = 2$

$2 + 7 = \underline{\ \ \ \ }$

5. $6 + 1 = \underline{\ \ \ \ }$

$\underline{\ \ \ \ } - 1 = 6$

6. $7 + 4 = \underline{\ \ \ \ }$

$\underline{\ \ \ \ } - 4 = 7$

7. $3 + 8 = \underline{\ \ \ \ }$

$11 - 8 = \underline{\ \ \ \ }$

8. $2 + \underline{\ \ \ \ } = 11$

$11 - 9 = \underline{\ \ \ \ }$

9. $3 + 2 = \underline{\ \ \ \ }$

$5 - \underline{\ \ \ \ } = 3$

10. $6 + \underline{\ \ \ \ } = 13$

$13 - 7 = \underline{\ \ \ \ }$

Make each number sentence true. Write + or −.

11. $13 \bigcirc 4 = 9$

$9 \bigcirc 4 = 13$

12. $9 \bigcirc 2 = 11$

$11 \bigcirc 2 = 9$

13. $6 \bigcirc 8 = 14$

$14 \bigcirc 8 = 6$

Draw a line to match the number sentences that show inverse operations.

14. $15 - 7 = 8$

15. $15 - 6 = 9$

16. $1 + 10 = 11$

17. $6 + 5 = 11$

a. $11 - 5 = 6$

b. $11 - 10 = 1$

c. $8 + 7 = 15$

d. $9 + 6 = 15$

Teacher Note: Use after Quick Check page 26 to reteach Unit 2, Lesson 2. **(4)**

Name _____

A **number sentence** tells how two or more numbers are related to each other. A number sentence can be true or false.

This number sentence is **true.**

$$4 + 6 = 10$$
$$10 = 10$$

Both sides of the equal sign have the same value.

This number sentence is **false.**

$$4 + 7 = 10$$

11 is not equal to **10**

The two sides of the equal sign have different values.

A letter is used as a **variable** to represent a number in a number sentence. The variable holds the place of a missing number. A number sentence with a variable is called an **open sentence.**

$4 + n = 10$ The letter *n* is used as a variable in this open sentence.

When *n* = **6**, the number sentence is true.

You can use a related number sentence to help you find the value of a variable.

$$3 + n = 12$$

Think: $12 - 3 = n$
$12 - 3 = 9$
$n = 9$

Write *true*, *false*, or *open*.

1. $10 - 3 = 8$

_____

2. $4 + 3 = 7$

_____

3. $13 - n = 8$

_____

4. $16 - 9 = 5$

_____

5. $9 + n = 12$

_____

6. $14 - 5 = 7$

_____

7. $9 + 6 = 14$

_____

8. $5 + 5 = 10$

_____

Find the value of *n* that makes the number sentence *true*.

9. $7 + n = 10$

$n =$ _____

10. $6 + n = 15$

$n =$ _____

11. $9 + n = 12$

$n =$ _____

12. $9 + n = 17$

$n =$ _____

13. $6 + n = 8$

$n =$ _____

14. $10 + n = 14$

$n =$ _____

15. $4 + n = 6$

$n =$ _____

16. $1 + n = 11$

$n =$ _____

Teacher Note: Use after Quick Check page 26 to reteach Unit 2, Lesson 3. **(4)**

Name _____

To estimate sums and differences, round each number to its greatest place value. Then add or subtract.

Estimate the sum **2,810 + 4,392**.

Round 4-digit numbers to the nearest thousand.

Th	H	T	O		
2,	8	1	0	→	3,000
+ 4,	3	9	2	→	+ 4,000

Find the estimated sum.

```
  3,000
+ 4,000
 ------
  7,000
```

Estimate the difference **487 − 212**.

Round 4-digit numbers to the nearest thousand.

H	T	O		
4	8	7	→	500
− 2	1	2	→	− 200

Find the estimated difference.

```
  500
− 200
 ----
  300
```

Estimate the sum or difference.

1. 84 → 80 / − 39 → − 40

2. 585 → 600 / + 146 → + 100

3. 8,235 → 8,000 / − 4,269 → − 4,000

4. 632 → 600 / + 313 → + ____

5. 482 → 500 / − 145 → − ____

6. 291 → 300 / + 681 → + ____

7. 143 → ____ / + 589 → + ____

8. 391 → ____ / − 282 → − ____

9. 907 → ____ / + 632 → + ____

10. 2,183 → ____ / − 1,421 → − ____

11. 3,521 → ____ / − 1,980 → − ____

12. 7,340 → ____ / − 3,049 → − ____

Teacher Note: Use after Quick Check page 32 to reteach Unit 2, Lesson 5. (4)

Name _____

Reteach 12

Money

Find the money amount.

- Order the bills and coins from greatest value to least value.
- Begin with the bill or coin of the greatest value.
- Add on the value of each bill or coin.

$5.00 $6.00 $6.25 $6.35 $6.45 $6.50

Write the money amount.

1.

$10.00 $15.00 $16.00   _____

2.

$.50 $.75 $.85   _____   _____   _____   _____

Write the money amounts. Circle the greater amount.

3.

_____   _____

4.

_____   _____

5.

_____   _____

Teacher Note: Use after Quick Check page 40 to reteach Unit 2, Lesson 9. **(4)**

Shaina gives the clerk a five-dollar bill for a total purchase of **$3.29.** What change should she receive?

To count change:

- Count on from the total purchase price.
- Begin with the bill or coin of the least value.
- Add on the value of each bill or coin until you reach the amount paid.

$3.29   **$3.30**   **$3.40**   **$3.50**   **$3.75**   **$4.00**   **$5.00**

To find the amount of change, count the money. Shaina should receive **$1.71** change.

Another way to find the change amount is to subtract.

You subtract money the same way you subtract whole numbers. Just make sure you line up the decimal points and include a dollar sign and decimal point in the answer.

$$\begin{array}{r} 4 \;\; \overset{9}{\cancel{10}} \;\; 10 \\ \$5.\cancel{0}\,\cancel{0} \\ -\;\; 3.2\;9 \\ \hline \$1.7\;1 \end{array}$$

Count the change.

1. Amount paid: **$2.00**

_____   _____   _____

---

2. Amount paid: **$10.00**

_____ _____ _____ _____ _____

Write the amount of change.

3. Paid: $3.25
   Price: − $3.05

4. Paid: $5.00
   Price: − $2.76

5. Paid: $8.52
   Price: − $1.37

Teacher Note: Use after Quick Check page 40 to reteach Unit 2, Lesson 10. (4)

Name _____

When you put **2** groups of **4** together, you make a group of **8**.

You can express this in different ways.

Addition sentence: **4 + 4 = 8**
Multiplication sentence: **2 × 4 = 8**

When you need to add numbers that are all the same, you can use multiplication.

3 + 3 + 3 + 3 = 12
↑   ↑   ↑   ↑
There are **4** threes. **4 × 3 = 12**

Complete.

1. ●●● ●●● ●●●
      ●● ●● ●●

5 + _____ + _____ = _____

_____ groups of **5** make _____

3 × _____ = _____

2. ●●● ●●● ●●● ●●●
      ●●● ●●● ●●● ●●●

6 + _____ + 6 + _____ = _____

4 groups of _____ make _____

4 × _____ = _____

3. ●●●● ●●●● ●●●●
      ●●● ●●● ●●●

7 + 7 + _____ = _____

_____ groups of **7** make _____

_____ × _____ = _____

4. ●●● ●●● ●●●
      ●●● ●●●

3 + _____ + _____ + _____ +

_____ = 15

5 groups of _____ make _____

_____ × _____ = _____

Complete the addition sentence. Then write a related multiplication sentence.

5. 4 + 4 + 4 + 4 = _____

_____

6. 3 + 3 + 3 = _____

_____

7. 7 + 7 + 7 + 7 = _____

_____

8. 5 + 5 + 5 + 5 + 5 = _____

_____

9. 6 + 6 + 6 = _____

_____

10. 2 + 2 + 2 + 2 + 2 + 2 = _____

_____

Teacher Note: Use before Unit 3, Lesson 1. **(4)**

You know that related addition and subtraction sentences make up fact families.

These sentences form an addition-subtraction fact family.

$8 + 4 = 12$ $4 + 8 = 12$ $12 - 4 = 8$ $12 - 8 = 4$

Related multiplication and division sentences also make up fact families.

You can use the **12 counters** in this array to show:

$3 \times 4 = 12$ and $4 \times 3 = 12$ and

$12 \div 3 = 4$ and $12 \div 4 = 3$.

These sentences form a multiplication-division fact family.

Use the arrays. Write a multiplication-division fact family.

1.

_____ × 6 = _____

_____ ÷ 6 = _____

6 × _____ = _____

_____ ÷ _____ = 6

2.

$3 \times 5 =$ _____

$15 \div$ _____ $= 3$

_____ × 3 = _____

_____ ÷ _____ = 5

Complete the sentences. Then write the missing multiplication and division sentences in the fact family.

3. $7 \times 3 =$ _____

$21 \div$ _____ $= 7$

$3 \times$ _____ $=$ _____

_____

4. $45 \div 5 =$ _____

$9 \times$ _____ $=$ _____

$5 \times$ _____ $=$ _____

_____

5. $8 \times 4 =$ _____

_____ _____

_____

6. $12 \div 6 =$ _____

_____ _____

_____

7. $63 \div 9 =$ _____

_____ _____

_____

8. $2 \times 7 =$ _____

_____ _____

_____

Teacher Note: Use before Unit 3, Lesson 1. **(4)**

Name _____

The Commutative Property of Multiplication means
that you can multiply factors in any order and you will
still get the same product.

2 groups of 3

$2 \times 3 = 6$

3 groups of 2

$3 \times 2 = 6$ So $2 \times 3 = 3 \times 2$.

The Associative Property of Multiplication means that
you can change how you group factors when you
multiply and you will still get the same product.

|| || || ||

 || ||

$2 \times (3 \times 2)$
$2 \times 6 = 12$
So $2 \times (3 \times 2) = (2 \times 3) \times 2$.

||| |||

||| |||

$(2 \times 3) \times 2$
$6 \times 2 = 12$

**Complete the multiplication sentence. Use the
commutative property.**

1. $4 \times 5 = $ _____ $\times 4$

2. $6 \times 3 = 3 \times$ _____

3. $6 \times$ _____ $= 4 \times 6$

4. _____ $\times 8 = 8 \times 5$

5. $7 \times 9 = $ _____ $\times$ _____

6. _____ $\times$ _____ $= 6 \times 5$

**Complete the multiplication sentence. Use the
associative property.**

7. $2 \times (3 \times 2) = (2 \times 3) \times$ _____

8. $4 \times (5 \times 2) = ($ _____ $\times 5) \times 2$

9. $6 \times (4 \times 3) = ($ _____ $\times 4) \times 3$

10. $(9 \times 2) \times$ _____ $= 9 \times (2 \times 4)$

11. $5 \times (2 \times 4) = $

    $($ _____ $\times$ _____ $) \times 4$

12. $(3 \times 5) \times 2 = 30$

    So $3 \times ($ _____ $\times$ _____ $) = $ _____.

13. $($ _____ $\times$ _____ $) \times 7 = $

    $2 \times (6 \times 7)$

14. $2 \times (8 \times 3) = $

    $($ _____ $\times$ _____ $) \times 3$

Teacher Note: Use after Quick Check page 52 to reteach Unit 3, Lesson 1. **(4)**

You can multiply money the same way you multiply whole numbers. Just remember to include a decimal point and a dollar sign in your answer.

- First, multiply the numbers.

- Then, count how many decimal places are in all the factors.

- Begin after the last digit in the product. Count that number of places from right to left.

- Put a decimal point at that place. Write the dollar sign.

Whole numbers	Decimals	
You know:	So:	
85 × 2 —— 170	$.85 × 2 —— $1.70	2 decimal places
135 × 3 —— 405	$1.35 × 3 —— $4.05	2 decimal places

Complete. Write any missing dollar signs, decimal points, or numbers.

1. $1.41
    ×   4
   ————
   $5 6 4

2. $3.56
    ×   5
   ————
   1 7 8 0

3. $1.49
    ×   6
   ————
   8 9 4

4. $4.37
    ×   3
   ————
   1 3 1 1

5. $.78
    ×   3

6. $.86
    ×   2

7. $1.93
    ×   4

8. $2.37
    ×   5

9. $.36
    ×   7

10. $.49
     ×   5

11. $2.19
     ×   6

12. $3.38
     ×   4

Teacher Note: Use after Quick Check page 60 to reteach Unit 3, Lesson 4. **(4)**

When you multiply by **10** or **100**, count the zeros
in the factors. The product has that many zeros.

$10 \times 1 = 10$

$10 \times 2 = 20$

Each pair
of factors
has **1** zero.

$10 \times 12 = 120$

Each product has **1** zero.

$10 \times 28 = 280$

$10 \times 314 = 3,140$

$10 \times 40 = 400$

$10 \times 400 = 4000$

Each pair
of factors
has **2** zeros.

$10 \times 80 = 800$

$10 \times 90 = 900$

Each pair
of factors
has **3** zeros.

$10 \times 500 = 5,000$

$100 \times 30 = 3,000$

$100 \times 3 = 300$

$10 \times 60 = 6,000$

$100 \times 7 = 700$

Each product
has **2** zeros.

Each product
has **3** zeros.

**Write how many zeros are in the pair of factors
and in the product.**

1.   13 _____ zero
        × 10

         _____ zero

2.   15 _____ zeros
        × 100

         _____ zeros

3.   50 _____ zeros
        × 10

         _____ zeros

4.   29 _____ zero
        × 10

         _____ zero

5.   20 _____ zeros
        × 10

         _____ zeros

6.   38 _____ zeros
        × 100

         _____ zeros

Multiply.

7.   80
        × 10

8.   150
        × 10

9.   24
        × 100

10.   820
         × 100

Teacher Note: Use after Quick Check page 60 to reteach Unit 3, Lesson 7. **(4)**

To estimate products, first round the factors.
Then, multiply the rounded numbers.

A number line can help you round.

Estimate the product: **33 × 18.**
Round each factor to the nearest ten.

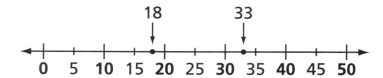

18 rounds up to **20**   18 →   20
33 rounds down to **30**   × 33 → × 30
                                                      600

The estimated product is **600.**

**Round each factor. Draw a number line if you
need help rounding.**

1.   32 →   30   **2.**   48 → _____   **3.**   26 → _____   **4.**   54 → _____
        × 46 → _____   × 53 →   50   × 37 → _____   × 29 → _____

**Round each factor. Draw a number line if you
need help rounding. Then multiply the rounded
factors to estimate the product.**

5.   39 → _____   **6.**   53 → _____   **7.**   72 → _____   **8.**   85 → _____
        × 16 → ×   20   × 67 → × _____   × 88 → × _____   × 49 → × _____

9.   39 → _____   **10.**   94 → _____   **11.**   35 → _____   **12.**   68 → _____
        × 16 → × _____   × 75 → × _____   × 25 → × _____   × 23 → × _____

Teacher Note: Use after Quick Check page 64 to reteach Unit 3, Lesson 8. **(4)**

How many groups of **2** are in **6**?

You can subtract groups of **2** from **6** exactly **3** times. There are **3** groups of **2**.

$$
\begin{array}{r} 6 \\ -\ 2 \\ \hline 4 \end{array}
\qquad
\begin{array}{r} 4 \\ -\ 2 \\ \hline 2 \end{array}
\qquad
\begin{array}{r} 2 \\ -\ 2 \\ \hline 0 \end{array}
$$

You can also show this as division.

$$
6 \div 2 = 3, \quad \text{or} \quad 2\overline{)6}^{\,3}
$$

$\uparrow$ dividend $\uparrow$ divisor $\uparrow$ quotient

Use repeated subtraction. Write the related division.

1. How many groups of **4** are in **12**?

$$
\begin{array}{r} 12 \\ -\ 4 \\ \hline \end{array}
\qquad
\begin{array}{r} 8 \\ -\ 4 \\ \hline \end{array}
\qquad
\begin{array}{r} 4 \\ -\ 4 \\ \hline \end{array}
$$

$12 \div 4 =$ _____

2. How many groups of **9** are in **18**?

$$
\begin{array}{r} 18 \\ -\ 9 \\ \hline \end{array}
\qquad
\begin{array}{r} 9 \\ -\ 9 \\ \hline \end{array}
$$

$18 \div$ _____ $=$ _____

3. How many groups of **8** are in **32**?

_____ $\div$ _____ $=$ _____

4. How many groups of **6** are in **18**?

_____ $\div$ _____ $=$ _____

Find the quotient.

5. $12 \div 2 =$ _____

6. $20 \div 5 =$ _____

7. $45 \div 5 =$ _____

8. $63 \div 9 =$ _____

9. $56 \div 8 =$ _____

10. $54 \div 6 =$ _____

11. $36 \div 6 =$ _____

12. $12 \div 6 =$ _____

13. $7 \div 1 =$ _____

14. $32 \div 4 =$ _____

15. $27 \div 9 =$ _____

16. $35 \div 5 =$ _____

17. $30 \div 6 =$ _____

18. $81 \div 9 =$ _____

19. $8 \div 8 =$ _____

Teacher Note: Use before Unit 4, Lesson 1. **(4)**

You can use division to help you find missing factors.

$n \times 4 = 32$

Find the value of **n**.

Think of a division fact that has the same numbers. $32 \div 4 = ?$ $32 \div 4 = n$	Complete the division fact. $32 \div 4 = 8$ $n = 8$	Replace the missing factor to check. $n \times 4 = 32$ $8 \times 4 = 32$ $n = 8$

Division rules can help you find the value of a variable.

- Zero divided by a number is zero. $0 \div 3 = n,\quad n = 0$
- A number divided by itself is **1**. $8 \div 8 = n,\quad n = 1$
- A number divided by **1** is the number. $6 \div 1 = n,\quad n = 6$

Write the related division fact. Then write the value of n.

1. $n \times 3 = 18$

$18 \div 3 = $ _____

$n = $ _____

2. $n \times 5 = 35$

_____ $\div$ _____ $=$ _____

$n = $ _____

Write the value of n. Use a division rule to help you.

3. $6 \div 6 = n$

$n = $ _____

4. $0 \div 7 = n$

$n = $ _____

5. $9 \div 1 = n$

$n = $ _____

6. $4 \div 4 = n$

$n = $ _____

Write the value of n.

7. $n \times 8 = 64$

$n = $ _____

8. $0 \div 8 = n$

$n = $ _____

9. $n \times 7 = 63$

$n = $ _____

10. $n \times 5 = 40$

$n = $ _____

11. $n \times 6 = 36$

$n = $ _____

12. $3 \div 1 = n$

$n = $ _____

13. $n \times 6 = 42$

$n = $ _____

14. $9 \div 9 = n$

$n = $ _____

You can use the order of operations to find the value of an expression.

| Remember: An expression is a combination of numbers and symbols that represents a quantity. |

Find the value: **2 + 3 × 5.**

| Check for parentheses.

2 + 3 × 5

There are no parentheses in this expression. | Multiply and divide from left to right.

2 + 3 × 5

2 + 15 | Add and subtract from left to right.

2 + 15 = 17

So 2 + 3 × 5 = 17. |

Use the order of operations to solve: **14 ÷ (2 + 5).**

| Check for parentheses. Do operations in parentheses first.

14 ÷ (2 + 5)

14 ÷ 7 | Multiply and divide from left to right.

14 ÷ 7 = 2

So 14 ÷ (2 + 5) = 2. |

Find the value of the expression. Use the order of operations.

1. 6 + 2 × 3

6 + _____ = _____

2. 12 ÷ 3 + 9

_____ + 9 = _____

3. 2 × 4 + 9

_____ + 9 = _____

4. 3 × (1 + 6)

3 × 7 = _____

5. 20 ÷ 5 − 1

_____ − 1 = _____

6. (9 − 2) × 8

_____ × 8 = _____

7. 10 ÷ (1 + 1)

10 ÷ _____ = _____

8. 18 − 9 ÷ 3

18 − _____ = _____

9. (4 + 1) × 6

_____ × 6 = _____

10. 4 + 1 × 6 _____

11. 8 ÷ 4 + 4 _____

12. 9 × (3 − 2) _____

13. (10 + 2) ÷ 4 _____

14. 6 − 2 ÷ 2 _____

15. 3 × 5 + 2 _____

16. 2 − 1 + 7 _____

17. 2 × 6 ÷ 3 _____

18. (3 − 1) × 9 _____

Teacher Note: Use after Quick Check page 80 to reteach Unit 4, Lesson 2. **(4)**

Find 3)‾14.

Draw a picture to show the division.

Circle as many groups of **3** as you can.

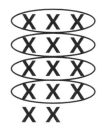

There are **4** groups of **3** with **2** left over.
The **2** left over is called the remainder.

Remember to include the quotient
and the remainder in your answer.

```
    4 R2
3)14
  − 12
    2
```

Use the picture to help you divide.

1.   R
2)7

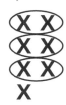

2.   R
3)8

3.   R
4)13

X X X X
X X X X
X X X X
X

Draw a picture. Divide.

4. 5)18

5. 3)16

6. 4)19

Divide.

7. 6)39   **8.** 5)47   **9.** 4)27   **10.** 9)73   **11.** 7)50

12. 3)10   **13.** 9)65   **14.** 7)30   **15.** 8)34   **16.** 8)46

Find **78 ÷ 4.**

Divide the tens.	Bring down the ones. Divide.	Write the remainder if there is one.

Divide the tens.

```
    Tens | Ones
       1 |
   4)  7 |  8
     - 4 |
   ------+----
       3 |
```

Multiply.
4 × 1 ten = 4 tens

Subtract. There are
3 tens left over.

Bring down the ones. Divide.

```
    Tens | Ones
       1 |  9
   4)  7 |  8
     - 4 |  ↓
   ------+----
       3 |  8
     - 3 |  6
   ------+----
         |  2
```

Multiply.
4 × 9 ones = 36 ones

Subtract. There are
2 ones left over.

Write the remainder if there is one.

```
    Tens | Ones
       1 |  9  R2
   4)  7 |  8
     - 4 |  ↓
   ------+----
       3 |  8
     - 3 |  6
   ------+----
         |  2
```

78 ÷ 4 = 19 R2

Complete.

1.
```
 Tens | Ones
   2)3 |  3
   - 2 |  ↓
  -----+----
    1  |  3
```

2.
```
 Tens | Ones
   3)3 |  7
   - 3 |  ↓
  -----+----
```

3.
```
 Tens | Ones
   4)8 |  6
   - 8 |
  -----+----
```

4.
```
 Tens | Ones
   2)7 |  7
   - 6 |
  -----+----
```

5.
```
 Tens | Ones
   5)6 |  9
```

6.
```
 Tens | Ones
   4)9 |  5
```

7.
```
 Tens | Ones
   3)9 |  4
```

8.
```
 Tens | Ones
   4)7 |  1
```

Divide.

9. 5)84　　　　**10.** 2)37　　　　**11.** 3)82　　　　**12.** 4)63

Teacher Note: Use after Quick Check page 88 to reteach Unit 4, Lesson 4. **(4)**

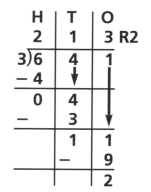

Find **641 ÷ 3**.

Divide the hundreds.

H	T	O
2		
3)6	4	1
− 6		
0		

Multiply.
3 × 2 hundreds = 6 hundreds
Subtract. There are
0 hundreds left over.

Bring down the tens. Divide.

H	T	O
2	1	
3)6	4↓	1
− 6		
0	4	
−	3	
	1	

Multiply.
3 × 1 tens = 3 tens

Subtract. There is
1 ten left over.

Bring down the ones. Divide.

H	T	O	
2	1	3	R2
3)6	4↓	1	
− 4		↓	
0	4		
−	3		
	1	1	
	−	9	
		2	

Multiply.
3 × 3 ones = 9 ones

Subtract. There are
2 ones left over.

641 ÷ 3 = 213 R2

Complete.

1.

H	T	O
1	5	
5)7	5↓	7↓
− 5		
2	5	
− 2	5	
	0	7

2.

H	T	O
1		
2)2	6↓	4
− 2		
0	6	

3.

H	T	O
1		
4)6	4↓	9
− 4		
2	4	

4.

H	T	O
7)8	6	1
− 7		

5.

H	T	O
6)7	8	7
− 6		

6.

H	T	O
8)9	9	3
− 8		

Divide.

7. 6)769

8. 3)459

9. 4)975

Find **612 ÷ 6**.

Divide the hundreds.	Bring down the tens. Divide.	Bring down the ones. Divide.

Divide the hundreds.

```
      H | T | O
      1 |   |
   6)6  | 1 | 2
    - 6 |   |
   ─────
      0 |   |
```

Multiply.
6 × 1 hundred = 6 hundreds
Subtract. There are **0 hundreds** left over.

Bring down the tens. Divide.

```
      H | T | O
      1 | 0 |
   6)6  | 1 | 2
    - 6 | ↓ |
   ─────
      0 | 1 |
```

There are not enough tens to divide. So write **0** in the tens place of the quotient.

Bring down the ones. Divide.

```
      H | T | O
      1 | 0 | 2
   6)6  | 1 | 2
    - 6 | ↓ | ↓
   ─────
      0 | 1 | 2
        -| 1 | 2
   ────────────
              0
```

Multiply.
6 × 2 ones = 12 ones
Subtract. There are **0 ones** left over.
There is no remainder.

612 ÷ 6 = 102

Complete.

1.
```
    H | T | O
    2 | 0 |
  3)6 | 2 | 7
   -6 | ↓ | ↓
  ──────────
    0 | 2 | 7
```

2.
```
    H | T | O
      | 8 |
  7)5 | 6 | 2
   -5 | 6 | ↓
  ──────────
    0 |   | 2
```

3.
```
    H | T | O
    1 | 0 |
  5)5 | 4 | 7
   -5 | ↓ | ↓
  ──────────
    0 | 4 | 7
```

4.
```
    H | T | O
    1 |   |
  8)8 | 6 | 9
   -8 |   |
```

5.
```
    H | T | O
      | 7 |
  3)2 | 2 | 1
   -2 | 1 |
```

6.
```
    H | T | O
      |   |
  5)9 | 5 | 3
   -5 |   |
```

Divide.

7. 6)638

8. 4)823

9. 6)785

Teacher Note: Use after Quick Check page 96 to reteach Unit 4, Lesson 7. **(4)**

Find **$3.72 ÷ 2**.

Divide as if you were dividing whole numbers.

```
    1 86
2)$3.72
  − 2
    1 7
  − 1 6
      12
    − 12
       0
```

Write the dollar sign and decimal point in the quotient.

```
   $1.86
2)$3.72
  − 2
    1 7
  − 1 6
      12
    − 12
       0
```

$3.72 ÷ 2 = $1.86

Complete.

1.
```
      1
6)$7.26
 − 6
   1 2
```

2.
```
      8
4)$3.56
 − 3 2
    36
```

3.
```
     1
5)$.95
 −5
```

4. 5)$5.95

5. 3)$9.15

6. 4)$.52

Divide.

7. 3)$7.83

8. 3)$6.96

9. 2)$8.14

Name _____

Reteach 28

Divisibility

Divisibility rules can help you decide whether one number evenly divides another number.

	Rule	Examples
Divisible by 2	The ones digit is **0, 2, 4, 6,** or **8.**	**24<u>8</u>** **45<u>4</u>**
Divisible by 3	The sum of the digits is divisible by **3.**	**471** **4 + 7 + 1 = 12** **12 ÷ 3 = 4** **471** is divisible by 3
Divisible by 5	The ones digit is **0** or **5.**	**65<u>5</u>** **70<u>0</u>**

Write which number is divisible by 2.

1. 1<u>6</u> 4<u>1</u> _____   **2.** 8<u>7</u> 24<u>0</u> _____   **3.** 62<u>1</u> 18<u>4</u> _____

4. 77 148 _____   **5.** 155 336 _____   **6.** 416 389 _____

Find the sum of the digits. Write *yes* if the number is divisible by 3. Write *no* if it is not.

7. 138   **8.** 87   **9.** 152   **10.** 431

1 + 3 + 8 = 12   8 + 7 = _____

_____   _____   _____   _____

Write the numbers that are divisible by 2.

11. 1<u>8</u> 8<u>0</u> 6<u>5</u> 1<u>3</u> 14<u>0</u>   **12.** 120 35 92 163 155

_____   _____

Complete the table. Write *yes* or *no* to tell whether the number is divisible by 2, 3, and 5.

	Divisible by 2	Divisible by 3	Divisible by 5
13. 60			
14. 75			
15. 255			
16. 567			

Teacher Note: Use after Quick Check page 96 to reteach Unit 4, Lesson 10. **(4)**

Copyright © Houghton Mifflin Company. All rights reserved.

Find **2,687 ÷ 5**.

Divide thousands.	Divide the thousands and hundreds.	Bring down tens. Divide.	Bring down ones. Divide.

Th	H	T	O
5)2,	6	8	7

There are not enough thousands.

	Th	H	T	O
		5		
5)	2,	6	8	7
−	2	5	↓	
		1		

Multiply.
5 × 5 hundreds = 25 hundreds
Subtract. There is **1 hundred** left over.

	Th	H	T	O
		5	3	
5)	2,	6	8	7
−	2	5	↓	
		1	8	
−		1	5	
			3	

Multiply.
5 × 3 tens = 15 tens
Subtract. There are **3 tens** left over.

	Th	H	T	O	
		5	3	7	R2
5)	2,	6	8	7	
−	2	5		↓	
		1	8		
−		1	5	↓	
			3	7	
−			3	5	
				2	

Multiply.
5 × 7 ones = 35 ones
Subtract. There are **2 ones** left over. Write the remainder.
2,687 ÷ 5 = 537 R2

Complete.

1.

Th	H	T	O
	9		
4)3	7	8	1
− 3	6	↓	
	1	8	

2.

Th	H	T	O
	6		
5)3	1	3	1
− 3	0	↓	
	1	3	

3.

Th	H	T	O
	9		
2)1	9	2	7
− 1	8	↓	
	1	2	

4.

Th	H	T	O
	8		
9)7	2	4	3
− 7	2		

5.

Th	H	T	O
	9		
6)5	7	9	3
− 5	4		

6.

Th	H	T	O
	5		
8)4	1	2	9
− 4	0		

Divide.

7. 3)2762

8. 7)4963

9. 6)5752

Name _____

Reteach 30

Averages

Find the average of this set of numbers:
14, 5, 20, and **17**.

Add the given numbers.	Count the addends.	Divide the sum by the number of addends.
14 5 20 + 17 — 56	14 → 1 5 → 2 20 → 3 + 17 → 4 — 56 **4 addends**	$\begin{array}{r} 14 \\ 4\overline{)56} \\ -\ 4 \\ \hline 16 \\ -\ 16 \\ \hline 0 \end{array}$ The average is **14**.

Complete to find the average of the set of numbers.

1. 7, 4, 10

$\begin{array}{r} 7 \\ 4 \\ +\ 10 \\ \hline 21 \end{array}$ 3)21

The average is _____ .

2. 14, 9, 10

$\begin{array}{r} 14 \\ 9 \\ +\ 10 \\ \hline 33 \end{array}$ 3)33

The average is _____ .

3. 22, 18, 27, 25

$\begin{array}{r} 22 \\ 18 \\ 27 \\ +\ 25 \end{array}$ 4)‾

The average is _____ .

4. 13, 22, 25

3)‾

+ __

The average is _____ .

5. 37, 46, 64

3)‾

+ __

The average is _____ .

6. 7, 16, 9, 20

4)‾

+ __

The average is _____ .

Find the average of the set of numbers.

7. 5, 19, 16, 8

The average is _____ .

8. 28, 39, 47

The average is _____ .

9. 60, 65, 88

The average is _____ .

Teacher Note: Use after Quick Check page 106 to reteach Unit 4, Lesson 14. **(4)**

Use models to compare fractions with like denominators.

Compare $\frac{1}{3}$ and $\frac{2}{3}$. These fractions have the same denominators.

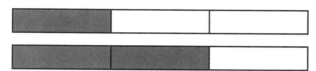

Both models show **3** equal parts. Compare the models. Which model shows less shading?

$\frac{1}{3}$ is less than $\frac{2}{3}$. $\frac{1}{3} < \frac{2}{3}$

Use the models to compare the fractions. Write < or >.

1.
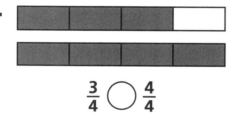
$$\frac{3}{4} \bigcirc \frac{4}{4}$$

2.
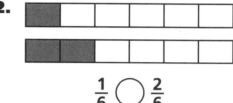
$$\frac{1}{6} \bigcirc \frac{2}{6}$$

3.
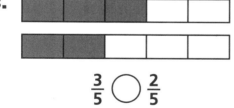
$$\frac{3}{5} \bigcirc \frac{2}{5}$$

4.
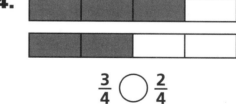
$$\frac{3}{4} \bigcirc \frac{2}{4}$$

5.
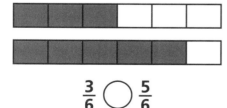
$$\frac{3}{6} \bigcirc \frac{5}{6}$$

6.
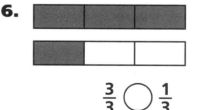
$$\frac{3}{3} \bigcirc \frac{1}{3}$$

Compare the fractions. Write < or >.

7. $\frac{1}{5} \bigcirc \frac{4}{5}$ **8.** $\frac{5}{6} \bigcirc \frac{4}{6}$ **9.** $\frac{4}{4} \bigcirc \frac{2}{4}$ **10.** $\frac{3}{6} \bigcirc \frac{1}{6}$

Teacher Note: Use before Unit 5, Lesson 1. **(4)**

Fractions that show the same amount are called **equivalent fractions.**

You can use models to show equivalent fractions.

Each of the models below is the same length, but has a different number of parts.

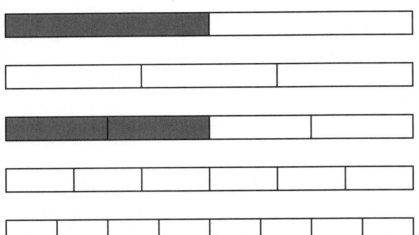

Find one equivalent fraction for $\frac{1}{2}$. You can see that $\frac{2}{4}$ shows the same amount as $\frac{1}{2}$. So $\frac{2}{4}$ is equivalent to $\frac{1}{2}$.

Write the equivalent fractions. You can shade the models above to help you.

1. Write three equivalent fractions for $\frac{1}{2}$. _____, _____, _____

2. Write an equivalent fraction for $\frac{2}{3}$. _____

3. Write an equivalent fraction for $\frac{3}{4}$. _____

4. Write an equivalent fraction for $\frac{1}{3}$. _____

5. Write five equivalent fractions for **1** whole.

_____, _____, _____, _____, _____

6. Write five equivalent fractions for **0.** _____, _____, _____, _____, _____

Teacher Note: Use after Quick Check page 116 to reteach Unit 5, Lesson 2. **(4)**

● You can compare fractions on a number line.

When you move to the left on the number line, the fractions decrease. When you move to the right, the fractions increase.

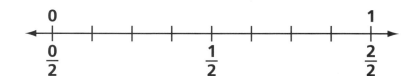

$\frac{1}{2}$ is less than $\frac{2}{2}$

$\frac{1}{2} < \frac{2}{2}$

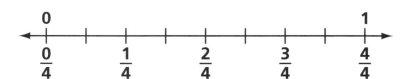

$\frac{3}{4}$ is greater than $\frac{1}{4}$

$\frac{3}{4} > \frac{1}{4}$

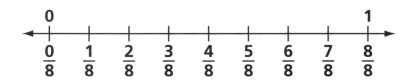

$\frac{2}{8}$ is equal to $\frac{1}{4}$

$\frac{2}{8} = \frac{1}{4}$

● **Write _is less than_, _is greater than_, or _is equal to_.**

1. $\frac{0}{2}$ _____ $\frac{1}{2}$ **2.** $\frac{3}{8}$ _____ $\frac{1}{8}$

Write <, >, or =.

3. $\frac{1}{8} \bigcirc \frac{6}{8}$ **4.** $\frac{2}{2} \bigcirc \frac{1}{2}$ **5.** $\frac{3}{4} \bigcirc \frac{2}{4}$ **6.** $\frac{2}{4} \bigcirc \frac{1}{4}$

7. $\frac{3}{8} \bigcirc \frac{5}{8}$ **8.** $\frac{4}{8} \bigcirc \frac{2}{4}$ **9.** $\frac{7}{8} \bigcirc \frac{2}{2}$ **10.** $\frac{3}{4} \bigcirc \frac{6}{8}$

Write the fractions in order from least to greatest.

11. $\frac{2}{8}, \frac{7}{8}, \frac{4}{8}, \frac{8}{8}, \frac{1}{8}$ _____, _____, _____, _____, _____

12. $\frac{1}{4}, \frac{2}{4}, \frac{0}{4}, \frac{3}{4}$ _____, _____, _____, _____

Name _____

Reteach 34

Estimating Fractions on a
Number Line

Estimate where to place $\frac{5}{8}$ on the number line.

You know that $\frac{1}{2}$ is equal to $\frac{4}{8}$. Mark $\frac{1}{2}$ on the number line.
Then divide each half into fourths.

Mark $\frac{5}{8}$ on the number line.

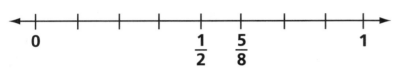

**Estimate where to place the fractions on the
number line.**

1. $\frac{1}{6}, \frac{3}{6}, \frac{5}{6}$

2. $\frac{2}{5}, \frac{3}{5}, \frac{4}{5}$

**Place the fractions on the number line. Then
order the fractions from least to greatest.**

3. $\frac{1}{8}, \frac{1}{4}, \frac{5}{8}, \frac{3}{4}$

_____

4. $\frac{6}{6}, \frac{2}{3}, \frac{5}{6}, \frac{3}{6}$

_____

5. Show where you would place $\frac{1}{4}$ and $\frac{3}{4}$ on the
number line in exercise **4**.

Teacher Note: Use after Quick Check page 120 to reteach Unit 5, Lesson 5. **(4)**

Copyright © Houghton Mifflin Company. All rights reserved.

These are **closed** figures.

These are **open** figures.

Line segments are straight.

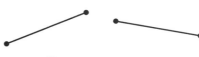

line segments

A **polygon** is a closed figure made up of line segments.

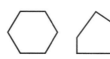

polygons

not polygons

A **triangle** has **3** sides.

A **rectangle** has **4** sides and **4** square corners.

A **square** has **4** sides all the same length and **4** square corners.

triangle

rectangle

square

Write *open* or *closed* for the figure.

1. _____

2. _____

3. _____

4. _____

Is the figure a polygon? Write *yes* or *no*.

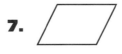

5. _____

6. _____

7. _____

8. _____

Write *triangle*, *rectangle*, or *square*.

9. _____

10. _____

11. _____

12. _____

Teacher Note: Use before Unit 6, Lesson 1. **(4)**

Point	Line	Line segment
•A	B—•—•C→	E•———————•F
Write: A	Write: $\overleftrightarrow{BC}$	Write: $\overline{EF}$
Read: Point A	Read: Line BC or line CB	Read: Line segment EF or line segment FE

Parallel line segments	Perpendicular line segments
L•———————•M R•———————•S	X•———•Y with •U on top, •V below
Write: $\overline{LM} \parallel \overline{RS}$	Write: $\overline{UV} \perp \overline{XY}$
Read: Line segment LM is parallel to line segment RS.	Read: Line segment UV is perpendicular to line segment XY.

Write *point, line,* or *line segment* for the figure.

1. •C

2. D
E

3. S R

4. •L
|
•M

_____ _____ _____ _____

Draw the figure.

5. $\overleftrightarrow{AB}$

6. point A

7. $\overline{MN}$

8. $\overleftrightarrow{RS}$

Write *parallel* or *perpendicular* for the pair of line segments.

9.
A D
C B

10.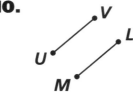
V
U L
M

_____ _____

Teacher Note: Use after Quick Check page 148 to reteach Unit 6, Lesson 1. **(4)**

Ray	Angle

Write: $\overrightarrow{AB}$	Write: ∠DEF or ∠FED or ∠E
Read: ray AB	Read: angle DEF or angle FED or angle E
A **ray** is part of a line. It has only 1 endpoint.	An **angle** is 2 rays that share the same endpoint.

A **right angle** is an angle that forms a square corner. To test whether an angle is a right angle, use the square corner of a piece of paper.

      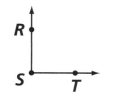

The angle is too big to be a right angle.   The angle is too small to be a right angle.   The angle is a right angle.

Write the name of the ray or angle.

1.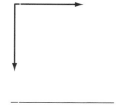

_____

2.

_____

3.

_____

4.

_____

Is the angle a right angle? Write *yes* or *no*.

5.

_____

6.

_____

7.

_____

8.

_____

Teacher Note: Use after Quick Check page 148 to reteach Unit 6, Lesson 2. **(4)**

Here's a way to test if two figures are congruent.

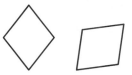

Trace one of the figures.

Put the traced figure over the other figure. You can turn the traced figure to make the parts match. If the figures match, they are congruent.

These two figures are congruent.

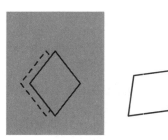

Are the figures congruent? Write *yes* or *no*.

1.

_____

2.

_____

3.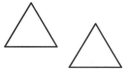

_____

4.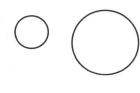

_____

Circle the letter of the figure that is congruent.

5.   **a.**   **b.**   **c.**

6.   **a.**   **b.**   **c.**

7.   **a.**   **b.**   **c.**

Teacher Note: Use after Quick Check page 148 to reteach Unit 6, Lesson 3. **(4)**

Type of angle	Picture	Measures
Right angle		Exactly **90°** A right angle forms a square corner.
Acute angle		Less than **90°**
Obtuse angle		Greater than **90°**

Name the angle. Write *right*, *acute*, or *obtuse*.

1.

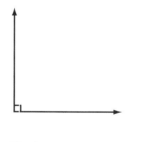

_____

2.

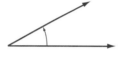

_____

3.

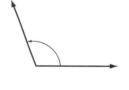

_____

4.

_____

5.

_____

6.

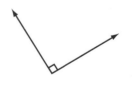

_____

7.

_____

8.

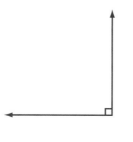

_____

9.

_____

Teacher Note: Use after Quick Check page 156 to reteach Unit 6, Lesson 5. **(4)**

Radius	Diameter

Write: $\overline{AB}$ or $\overline{BA}$	Write: $\overline{CB}$ or $\overline{BC}$
Read: radius *AB* or radius *BA*	Read: diameter *BC* or diameter *CB*

A figure can be turned a fraction of a circle.

A turn of **90°** is a one-quarter turn.	A turn of **180°** is a half turn.	A turn of **270°** is a three-quarter turn.	A turn of **360°** is a full turn.
 90°	 180°	270°	360°

Write *radius* or *diameter* to name the dotted segment.

1.

_____

2.

_____

3.

_____

4.

_____

Name the turn.

5. 180°

_____

6. 270°

_____

7. 360°

_____

8. 90°

_____

Teacher Note: Use after Quick Check page 156 to reteach Unit 6, Lesson 6. **(4)**

Name _____

Reteach 41

Symmetry

These figures each have a **line of symmetry.** If you fold the figure along a line of symmetry, the parts match.

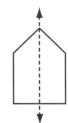 

This figure has **rotational symmetry.** You can rotate or spin it less than a full turn, and it looks the same.

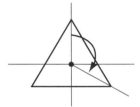 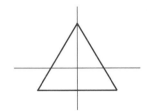

Is the dotted line a line of symmetry? Write *yes* or *no*.

1.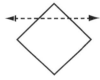

2.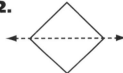

3.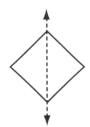

4.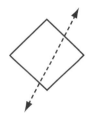

_____ _____ _____ _____

5.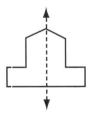

6.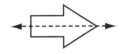

7.

8.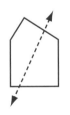

_____ _____ _____ _____

Does the figure have rotational symmetry? Write *yes* or *no*.

9.

10.

11.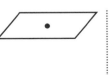

12.

_____ _____ _____ _____

Reteach Worksheets

Teacher Note: Use after Quick Check page 156 to reteach Unit 6, Lesson 7. **(4)**

equilateral triangle	isosceles triangle	scalene triangle
all sides are the same length	two sides are the same length	each side is a different length

Write whether the triangle is *equilateral, isosceles,* or *scalene.*

1.

two sides the
same length

_____

2.

all sides the
same length

_____

3.

each side a
different length

_____

4.

_____

5.

_____

6.

_____

7.

_____

8.

_____

9.

_____

10.

_____

11.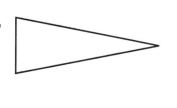

_____

12.

_____

Teacher Note: Use after Quick Check page 160 to reteach Unit 6, Lesson 8. **(4)**

You can use the number of angles to name polygons.

3 angles — **triangle**   5 angles — **pentagon**
4 angles — **quadrilateral**   6 angles — **hexagon**

These quadrilaterals all have special names.

Name	Picture	Description
square		4 right angles 4 sides the same length
rhombus		4 sides the same length
trapezoid		1 pair of parallel sides
rectangle		4 right angles 2 pairs of parallel sides
parallelogram		2 pairs of parallel sides

Name the polygon. Write *triangle, quadrilateral, pentagon,* or *hexagon.*

1.

_____

2.

_____

3.

_____

4.

_____

Write the special name for the quadrilateral.

5.

_____

6.

_____

7.

_____

8.

_____

9.

_____

10.

_____

11.

_____

12.

_____

Teacher Note: Use after Quick Check page 160 to reteach Unit 6, Lesson 9. **(4)**

Name _____

Reteach 44

Space Figures

Space Figure	Description	Picture
cube	6 flat faces 8 vertices (1 is called a vertex)	
rectangular prism	6 flat faces 8 vertices	
rectangular pyramid	5 flat faces 5 vertices	
cylinder	2 flat faces 2 edges	
cone	1 vertex 1 flat face	
sphere	0 vertices 0 flat faces	

Name the space figure. Write the number of flat faces.

1. _____ faces

_____

2. _____ faces

_____

3. _____ faces

_____

4.

_____

_____ faces

5.

_____ faces

6.

_____ faces

Teacher Note: Use after Quick Check page 166 to reteach Unit 6, Lesson 10. **(4)**

A **net** is a pattern for a space figure. To make a space figure from a net, follow these steps.

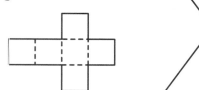

Trace the net. Then cut along the solid line.

Fold along the dotted lines.

Tape the figure together.

Trace the net and make the space figure shown.

1.

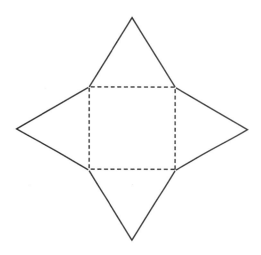

2.

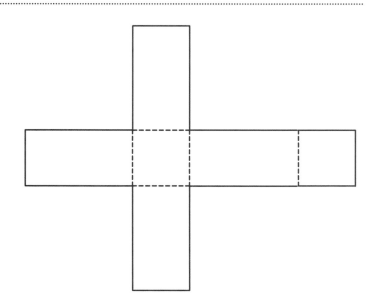

Teacher Note: Use after Quick Check page 166 to reteach Unit 6, Lesson 11. **(4)**

Name _____

One end of the paper clip is at the **0** mark on the ruler. The other end is between $1\frac{1}{2}$ inches and **2** inches. It is closer to **2** inches. The paper clip is about **2** inches long.

Measure to the nearest half inch.

1. About how long is the pencil?

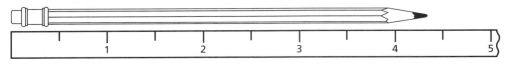

between **4** and $4\frac{1}{2}$ inches   about _____ inches

2. About how long is the eraser?

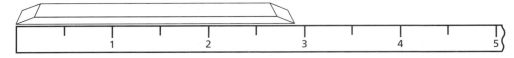

between $2\frac{1}{2}$ and _____ inches   about _____ inches

3. About how long is the key?

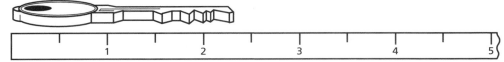

between _____ and _____ inches

about _____ inches

4. About how long is stapler?

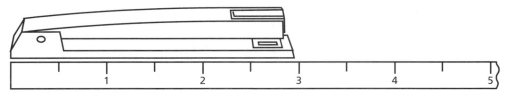

between _____ and _____ inches

about _____ inches

Teacher Note: Use before Unit 7, Lesson 1. **(4)**

The **perimeter** of a figure is the distance around the figure. To find the perimeter of a figure shown on a grid, you can count units. One edge of a grid square counts as **1** unit. Count units along the sides of the figure.

Count the units around the rectangle. Remember to count only the units along each side. The perimeter of the rectangle is **10** units.

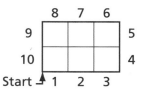

Find the perimeter of each figure.

1.
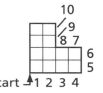

Perimeter: _____ units

2.
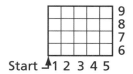

Perimeter: _____ units

3.
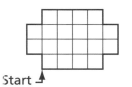

Perimeter: _____ units

4.
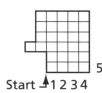

Perimeter: _____ units

5.
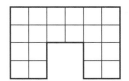

Perimeter: _____ units

6.

Perimeter: _____ units

7.

Perimeter: _____ units

8.

Perimeter: _____ units

The **area** of a figure is the number of **square units** needed to cover the figure. To find the area of a figure shown on a grid, count the number of grid squares inside the figure. Each grid square is **1** square unit.

This is **1** square unit. → ☐

The rectangle is covered by **8** grid squares. The area is **8** square units.

1	3	5	7
2	4	6	8

Count the squares. Write the area.

1.

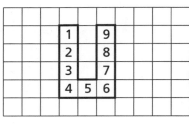

_____ square units

2.

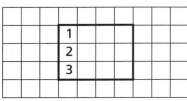

_____ square units

3.

_____ square units

4.

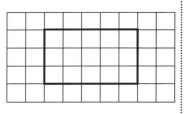

_____ square units

5.

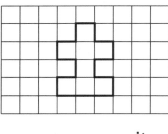

_____ square units

6.

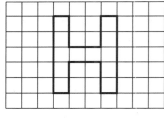

_____ square units

7.

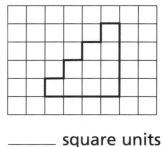

_____ square units

8.

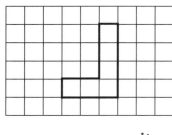

_____ square units

9.

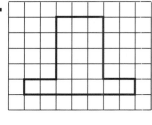

_____ square units

Teacher Note: Use before Unit 7, Lesson 1. **(4)**

A **cubic unit** is a cube that is **1** unit on each edge. The number of cubic units needed to fill all the space inside a rectangular prism is the **volume** of the rectangular prism. You can find the volume of a rectangular prism by counting cubes.

This is **1** cubic unit.

Count the cubes in this rectangular prism. Start with the top layer. It has **3** rows of **3** cubes, or **9** cubes. There are **3** layers of cubes. **3 × 9** cubes = **27** cubes. The volume is **27** cubic units.

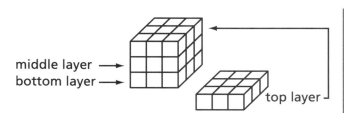

middle layer →
bottom layer →
top layer ⌐

Find the volume of each rectangular prism.

1.

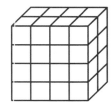

There are **8** cubic units in the top layer.

There are **4** layers.

Total: _____ cubic units

2.

There are **8** cubic units in the top layer.

There are _____ layers.

Total: _____ cubic units

3.

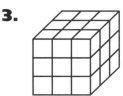

There are _____ cubic units in the top layer.

There are _____ layers.

Total: _____ cubic units

4.

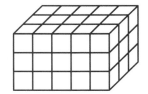

There are _____ cubic units in the top layer.

There are _____ layers.

Total: _____ cubic units

5.

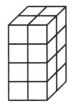

There are _____ cubic units in the top layer.

There are _____ layers.

Total: _____ cubic units

6.

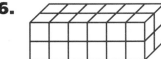

There are _____ cubic units in the top layer.

There are _____ layers.

Total: _____ cubic units

Teacher Note: Use before Unit 7, Lesson 1. **(4)**

Name _____

The distance between any number on the ruler and the
next number is **1 centimeter (1 cm)**. The distance
between any small mark and the next mark is
1 millimeter (1 mm). There are **10** mm in **1** cm.

The short line segment above the ruler measures **8 mm**.
The long line segment above the ruler measures **3 cm**.

Write the length of the line segment in cm.

1.

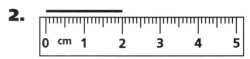

_____ cm

2.

_____ cm

Write the length of the line segment in mm.

3.

_____ mm

4.

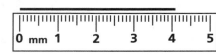

_____ mm

Use the equivalent measures: 1 cm = 10 mm.
Complete.

5. 3×1 cm = 3×10 mm, or _____ mm

6. 4 cm = $4 \times$ _____ mm, or _____ mm

7. 6 cm = _____ $\times 10$ mm, or _____ mm

8. 8 cm = _____ $\times$ _____ mm, or _____ mm

9. 5 cm = _____ mm   **10.** 9 cm = _____ mm

11. 2 cm = _____ mm   **12.** 7 cm = _____ mm

Teacher Note: Use after Quick Check page 180 to reteach Unit 7, Lesson 1. **(4)**

These are equivalent
metric lengths.

10 centimeters (cm) = **1** decimeter (dm)
10 dm = **1** meter (m)
100 cm = **1** m
1,000 m = **1** kilometer (km)

Draw lines to match with the best estimate.

1. the height of a tall tree   **10 km**

2. the distance you might ride
your bike in **1** hour   **10 cm**

3. the length of a spoon   **10 m**

Complete.

4. Since **1 dm = 10 cm**, then **8 dm = 8 × 10 cm**, or _____ cm.

5. Since **1 km = 1,000 m**, then **7 km = 7 × 1,000 m**, or _____ m.

6. Since **1 m = 100 cm**, then **5 m =** _____ **× 100 cm**, or _____ cm.

7. Since **1 m = 10 dm**, then **4 m =** _____ **×** _____ dm, or _____ dm.

8. Since **90 cm = 9 dm**, then **40 cm =** _____ dm.

9. Since **4,000 m = 4 km**, then **8,000 m =** _____ km.

10. Since **600 cm = 6 m**, then **900 cm =** _____ m.

11. Since **20 dm = 2 m**, then **40 dm =** _____ m.

12. 3 dm = _____ cm   **13.** 5 km = _____ m   **14.** 3 m = _____ cm

15. 7 m = _____ dm   **16.** 50 m = _____ cm   **17.** 30 km = _____ m

Teacher Note: Use after Quick Check page 180 to reteach Unit 7, Lesson 2. **(4)**

Liters and milliliters are metric measures of liquid capacity. 1 liter (L) = **1,000** milliliters (mL)	Grams and kilograms are metric measures of mass. 1 kilogram (kg) = **1,000** grams (g)

When you change a measurement in smaller units to an equivalent measurement in larger units, there will be fewer of the larger units.

When you change a measurement in larger units to an equivalent measurement in smaller units, there will be more of the smaller units.

**Write *larger* or *smaller* to describe the new unit.
Then write *more* or *fewer* to describe the
number of new units.**

1. 3 L = ? mL

_____

_____

2. 5,000 g = ? kg

_____

_____

3. 6,000 mL = ? L

_____

_____

4. 7 kg = ? g

_____

_____

Write the equivalent measure of liquid capacity.

5. 4 L = _____ mL

6. 1,500 mL = _____ L

7. 2,500 mL = _____ L

8. $3\frac{1}{2}$ L = _____ mL

9. 4,500 mL = _____ L

10. 8,000 mL = _____ L

Write the equivalent measure of mass.

11. 3,000 g = _____ kg

12. 9 kg = _____ g

13. $1\frac{1}{2}$ kg = _____ g

14. 5,500 g = _____ kg

15. 8,000 g = _____ kg

16. 6 kg = _____ g

Teacher Note: Use after Quick Check page 180 to reteach Unit 7, Lesson 3. **(4)**

Name _____

The Celsius thermometer shows **0°**
when water freezes and **100°**
when water boils.

This thermometer shows **25° C.**
This could be the temperature
outside on a warm day.

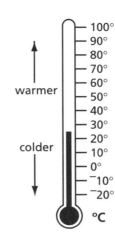

**Write whether the temperature is *warmer* or
cooler than 25°C.**

1. 0° C

2. 20° C

3. 70° C

_____   _____   _____

**Write the temperature shown on the
thermometer.**

4.
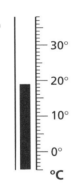

_____

5.
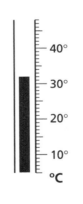

_____

6.

_____

7.
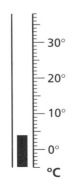

_____

8.
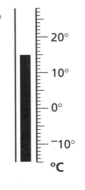

_____

9.
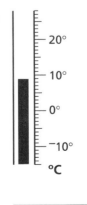

_____

Teacher Note: Use after Quick Check page 188 to reteach Unit 7, Lesson 4. **(4)**

Name _____

Customary Units of Length:
Inch, Half Inch, Quarter Inch

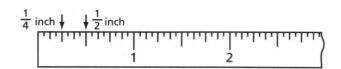

$\frac{1}{4}$ inch ↓   ↓ $\frac{1}{2}$ inch

Measure to the nearest quarter inch.

1.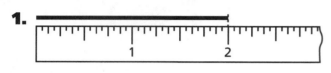

_____

2.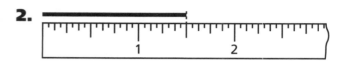

_____

3.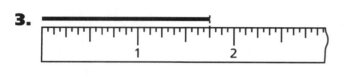

_____

4.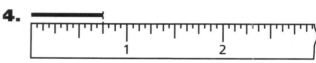

_____

5.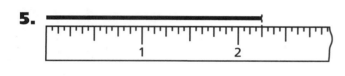

_____

6.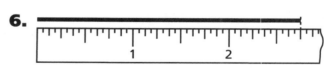

_____

Measure the line segment. Write the letter of the correct measurement.

7. _____

a. **3** in.

8. _____

b. $2\frac{3}{4}$ in.

9. _____

c. $1\frac{1}{2}$ in.

10. _____

d. $3\frac{1}{4}$ in.

Teacher Note: Use after Quick Check page 188 to reteach Unit 7, Lesson 6. **(4)**

Feet, yards, and miles are customary units of length.

| A sheet of paper is about **1** foot long. | A door is about **1** yard wide. | You can walk about **1** mile in **20** minutes. |

Draw lines to match the item with an appropriate measurement.

1. the distance between cities **4 feet**

2. the height of a mailbox **4 yards**

3. the height of a flagpole **4 miles**

Circle the customary unit you would use to measure each item.

4. the height of a tree

feet   miles

5. the length of a house

miles   yards

6. the distance walked in an hour

miles   feet

Write *feet, yards,* or *miles*.

7. A plane flying is **5** _____ high.

8. The chalkboard is **3** _____ long.

9. A third grader is **4** _____ tall.

10. A table is $2\frac{1}{2}$ _____ high.

Use the table to complete equivalent measurements.

Inches	12	24	36	48	60	72	84	96
Feet	1	2	3	4	5	6	7	8
Yards			1			2		

11. 1 yd = _____ in.

12. 4 ft = _____ in.

13. 72 in. = _____ yd

14. 6 ft = _____ yd

15. 24 in. = _____ ft

16. 5 ft = _____ in.

17. 2 yd = _____ ft

18. 48 in. = _____ ft

19. 7 ft = _____ in.

Teacher Note: Use after Quick Check page 188 to reteach Unit 7, Lesson 7. **(4)**

Cups, pints, quarts, and **gallons** are customary
units of liquid capacity.

	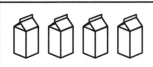	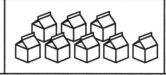	

1 gallon (gal) = **4** quarts (qt) = **8** pints (pt) = **16** cups (c)

1 quart = **2** pints = **4** cups

Ounces and **pounds** are customary units of weight.
1 pound = **16** ounces (oz)

Complete the table.

1.

Cups	2	4	6	8	10			
Pints	1	2	3	4				

2.

Pints	8	16	24	32				
Quarts	4	8	12	16				
Gallons	1	2	3					

Use the tables to complete.

3. 2 c = _____ pt   **4.** 8 pt = _____ qt   **5.** 2 gal = _____ pt

Complete the table.

6.

Pounds	1	2	3	4		
Ounces	16	32	48			

Use the table to complete.

7. 1 lb = _____ oz   **8.** 2 lb = _____ oz   **9.** 48 oz = _____ lb

Teacher Note: Use after Quick Check page 197 to reteach Unit 7, Lesson 8. **(4)**

The thermometer is like a number line that goes up and down instead of right and left.

The numbers below **0** are negative numbers (−). The numbers above **0** are positive numbers (+). You do not have to use a + sign to show a positive number, but you must use a − sign to show a negative number.

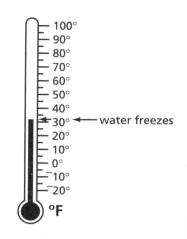

←— water freezes

°F

Circle the colder temperature.

1. 34°F or 25°F   **2.** ⁻6°F or ⁻4°F   **3.** 16°F or 24°F

4. 35°F or 32°F   **5.** 7°F or 9°F   **6.** ⁻1°F or ⁻5°F

7. 10°F or ⁻20°F   **8.** 0°F or 2°F   **9.** 0°F or ⁻10°F

Circle the letter that describes the temperature.

10. 32°F

    a. water boils

    b. water freezes

11. 5°F

    a. above freezing

    b. below freezing

12. 0°F

    a. a very warm day

    b. a very cold day

Write the temperature. Use the thermometer if you need to.

13. The temperature was **70°F** and increased **20°F**.

    What was the new temperature? _____

    Would you go skiing or to the beach? _____

14. The temperature was **50°F** and decreased **25°**.

    What was the new temperature? _____

    Was it warmer or colder than before? _____

15. What temperature is **10°** warmer than ⁻**10°F**? _____

16. What temperature is **5°** colder than ⁻**5°F**? _____

Teacher Note: Use After Quick Check page 197 to reteach Unit 7, Lesson 9. (4)   **115**

The **perimeter** of a figure is the distance around it. Find the perimeter of any shape by adding the lengths of its sides. Use *P* to stand for the perimeter.

To find the perimeter of the triangle, add the lengths of the three sides.
P = **4** m + **3** m + **5** m = **12** m

The perimeter of the triangle is **12** meters.

If some sides of a figure are the same length, you can use multiplication to help you find the perimeter.

To find the perimeter of a square, multiply the length of a side (*s*) by **4**.

$P = 4 \times s$
$P = 4 \times 5$ cm
$P = 20$ cm

The perimeter of the square is **20** centimeters.

To find the perimeter of a rectangle, add the length (*l*) and the width (*w*), and multiply the sum by **2**.

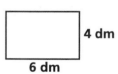

$P = 2 \times (l + w)$
$P = 2 \times (6$ dm $+ 4$ dm$)$
$P = 2 \times 10$ dm $= 20$ dm

The perimeter of the rectangle is **20** decimeters.

Find the perimeter.

1.

4 yards | 8 yards

4 yd + **8** yd

= **12** yd

2 × **12** yd = _____

P = _____ yd

2.

8 in | 11 m | 5 in

8 in. + **5** in. + **11** in. = _____ in.

P = _____ in.

3.

7 cm | 7 cm

4 × **7** cm = _____

P = _____

4.

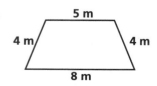

P = _____

Teacher Note: Use after Quick Check page 197 to reteach Unit 7, Lesson 11. **(4)**

The area of a figure is the number of square units the figure covers. In this rectangle, each square stands for **1** square cm.

You can find the area by counting the squares. There are **15** squares. The area is **15** square cm.

Length × Width = Area

5 cm × 3 cm = 15 square cm

You can also find the area by multiplying the length times the width.

Area (A) = Length (l) × Width (w)

Find the area.

1.

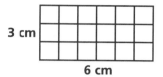

3 cm
6 cm

3 cm × **6** cm = _____ square cm

A = _____ square cm

2.

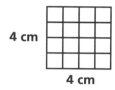

4 cm
4 cm

4 cm × **4** cm = _____ square cm

A = _____ square cm

3.

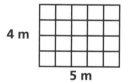

4 m
5 m

A = _____

4.

3 cm A =

A = _____

5.

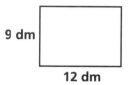

9 dm
12 dm

9 dm × **12** dm = _____

A = _____

6.

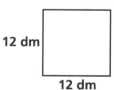

12 dm
12 dm

12 dm × **12** dm = _____

A = _____

7.

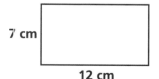

7 cm
12 cm

A = _____

8.

9 m

A = _____

Teacher Note: Use after Quick Check page 202 to reteach Unit 7, Lesson 12. **(4)**

Name _____

You can find the perimeter of this figure by adding the
lengths of the sides.

2 in. + 2 in. + 3 in. + 4 in. + 5 in. + 6 in. = 22 in.

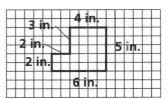

You can find the area of the figure by dividing it into
two rectangles.

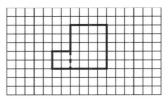

Find the area of each rectangle.
$A = l \times w$ $A = l \times w$
$A = $ **2** in. × **2** in. $A = $ **4** in. × **5** in.
$A = $ **4** square in. $A = $ **20** square in.

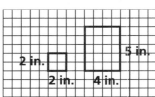

Then add the areas to find the total area.
4 square in. + 20 square in. = 24 square in.

Find the perimeter and area.

1.

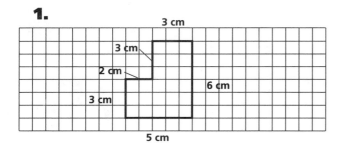

3 cm + 6 cm + 5 cm +
3 cm + 2 cm + 3 cm + _____

2.

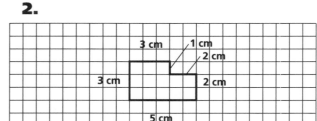

$P = $ _____ m

3.

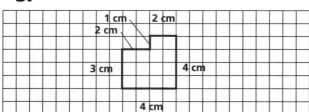

$P = $ _____

$A = $ _____

4.

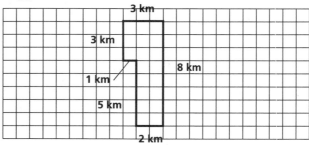

$P = $ _____

$A = $ _____

Teacher Note: Use after Quick Check page 202 to reteach Unit 7, Lesson 13. **(4)**

To find the **surface area** of a rectangular prism, add the areas of all **6** faces.

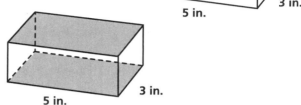

Two faces are **5** in. × **3** in.
2 × (5 × 3) = 2 × 15 = 30 square in.

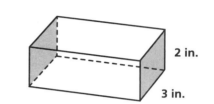

Two faces are **2** in. × **3** in.
2 × (2 × 3) = 2 × 6 = 12 square in.

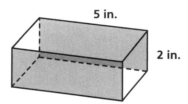

Two faces are **5** in. × **2** in.
2 × (5 × 2) = 2 × 10 = 20 square in.

30 + 12 + 20 = 62 square in.
The surface area of the rectangular prism is
62 square inches.

Find the surface area of the rectangular prism.

1.

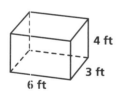

2 × (6 × 3) = _____

2 × (3 × 4) = _____

2 × (6 × 4) = _____

Surface Area _____

2.

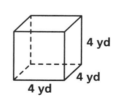

6 × _____ × _____ = _____

Surface Area _____

3.

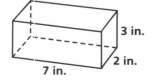

Surface Area _____

4.

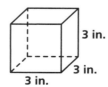

Surface Area _____

Teacher Note: Use after Quick Check page 206 to reteach Unit 7, Lesson 14. **(4)**

The **volume** of a space figure is the amount of space inside. Volume is measured in **cubic units.** The volume of this rectangular prism is **36** cubic units.

You can find the volume (V) of this rectangular prism by counting cubes. You could also find the volume by multiplying the length (*l*) times the width (*w*) times the height (*h*).

3 units

4 units

3 units

$$V = l \times w \times h$$
$$V = 4 \times 3 \times 3$$
$$V = 36 \text{ cubic units}$$

Find the volume.

1.

2 × 2 × 2 = _____

V = _____ cubic cm

2.

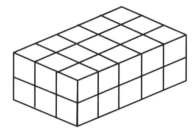

3 × _____ × _____ = _____

V = _____ cubic cm

3.

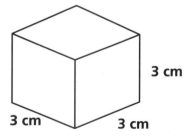

3 cm

3 cm   3 cm

V = _____ cubic cm

4.

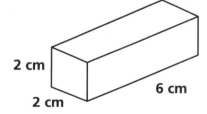

2 cm

2 cm

6 cm

V = _____ cubic cm

5.

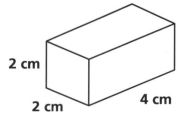

2 cm

2 cm   4 cm

V = _____ cubic cm

6.

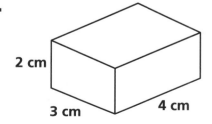

2 cm

3 cm   4 cm

V = _____ cubic cm

Teacher Note: Use after Quick Check page 206 to reteach Unit 7, Lesson 15. **(4)**

The square is divided into **10** equal parts. Each part is one tenth of the whole square. There are **3** shaded parts.

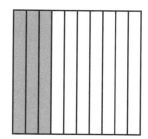

You can show the part of the whole square that is shaded in words,   as a fraction,   or as a decimal.
↓   ↓   ↓

three tenths $\frac{3}{10}$ 0.3

$$\text{three tenths} = \frac{3}{10} = 0.3$$

Write the number in words, as a fraction, and as a decimal.

	Decimal Model	Words	Fraction	Decimal
1.		nine tenths	$\frac{\ }{10}$	0.___
2.				
3.				
4.				
5.				
6.				
7.				
8.				

Teacher Note: Use before Unit 8, Lesson 1. **(4)**

Name _____

Each square is **1** whole. When a whole is divided into **10** equal parts, each part is **1** tenth. The whole is **10** tenths.

The shaded parts of the model are **2** whole squares and **7** of the **10** tenths. So the model shows two and seven tenths.

You can show the shaded part

in words,	as a mixed number,	or as a decimal.
↓	↓	↓
two and seven tenths	$2\frac{7}{10}$	2.7

$$\text{two and seven tenths} = 2\frac{7}{10} = 2.7$$

Write a mixed number and a decimal for the shaded region.

1. 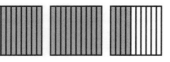   **2.** 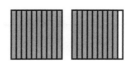   **3.**

_____   _____   _____

_____   _____   _____

Write each fraction or mixed number as a decimal.

4. $\frac{5}{10} =$ _____   **5.** $1\frac{4}{10} =$ _____   **6.** $2\frac{3}{10} =$ _____

7. $\frac{8}{10} =$ _____   **8.** $3\frac{1}{10} =$ _____   **9.** $2\frac{7}{10} =$ _____

Write each decimal as a fraction or mixed number.

10. 0.9 = _____   **11.** 2.4 = _____   **12.** 1.5 = _____

13. 3.3 = _____   **14.** 2.8 = _____   **15.** 4.9 = _____

Teacher Note: Use after Quick Check page 218 to reteach Unit 8, Lesson 1. **(4)**

Each square is **1** whole. When a whole is divided into **100** equal parts, each part is one hundredth. The whole is **100** hundredths.

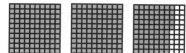

The shaded parts of the model are **2** whole squares and **75** of the **100** hundredths. So the model shows two and seventy-five hundredths.

You can show the shaded part in words,

↓

two and seventy-five hundredths

as a mixed number,

↓

$2\frac{75}{100}$

or as a decimal.

↓

2.75

two and seventy-five hundredths = $2\frac{75}{100}$ = 2.75

Write the letter of the matching number words.

1. 0.3 _____   a. one and five tenths

2. 1.05 _____   b. three hundredths

3. 0.03 _____   c. one and nine hundredths

4. 1.9 _____   d. one and five hundredths

5. 1.5 _____   e. three tenths

6. 1.09 _____   f. one and nine tenths

Write a decimal and a fraction or mixed number.

7. eight tenths

_____

10. seven hundredths

_____

_____

8. two and three tenths

_____

11. fourteen hundredths

_____

_____

9. four and four hundredths

_____

12. three and six hundredths

_____

_____

Write each decimal in words.

13. 0.15 _____

14. 3.35 _____

Name _____

You can use models to compare decimals.
The models show **0.3** and **0.30**.
The same amounts are shaded, so **0.3 = 0.30**,
or **0.3** is equivalent to **0.30**.

3 of 10   30 of 100
equal parts   equal parts

Compare **1.43** and **1.41**.

Ones	.	Tenths	Hundredths
1	.	4	3
1	.	4	1

You can also use place value to compare
decimals. Start at the left. If the whole
numbers are the same, compare the tenths
digits. If the tenths digits are the same,
compare the hundredths digits.

Think: **1 = 1**   Think: **4 = 4**   Think: **3 > 1**

So, **1.43 > 1.41.**

Write an equivalent decimal.

1. 0.4 = 0. _____

2. 0.60 = 0. _____

3. 0.90 = _____

4. 1.5 = _____

5. 3.80 = _____

6. 8.30 = _____

Compare. Write >, <, or =.

7.

Ones	.	Tenths	Hundredths
1	.	6	7
1	.	7	

1.67 ◯ 1. 7

8.

Ones	.	Tenths	Hundredths
2	.	4	
2	.	4	0

2.4 ◯ 2.40

9. 4.23 ◯ 4.3

10. 5.41 ◯ 5.38

11. 0.79 ◯ 0.8

12. 6.39 ◯ 6.04

Teacher Note: Use after Quick Check page 218 to reteach Unit 8, Lesson 3. **(4)**

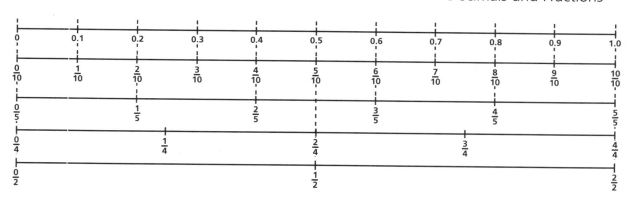

To find the equivalent decimal for a fraction:

1. Rewrite the fraction with a denominator of **10** or **100**.

2. Then write the fraction as a decimal.

$$\frac{1}{4} \times \frac{?}{?} = \frac{?}{100}$$ Think: **4 × 25 = 100**

$$\frac{1}{4} \times \frac{25}{25} = \frac{25}{100} \rightarrow 0.25$$

So, $\frac{1}{4} = 0.25$

Write each fraction as an equivalent fraction that has a denominator of 10 or 100.

1. $\frac{1}{2} = \frac{}{10}$

Think: **2 × 5 = 10**

2. $\frac{3}{4} = \frac{}{100}$

Think: **4 × 25 = 100**

and **3 × 25 = _____**

3. $\frac{1}{5} =$ _____

Think: **5 × 2 = 10**

4. $\frac{1}{25} =$ _____

5. $\frac{7}{20} =$ _____

6. $\frac{4}{50} =$ _____

Write the decimal for each fraction or mixed number.

7. $2\frac{1}{2} =$ _____

8. $1\frac{3}{4} =$ _____

9. $3\frac{4}{5} =$ _____

10. $\frac{4}{5} =$ _____

11. $\frac{9}{50} =$ _____

12. $5\frac{3}{20} =$ _____

Reteach Worksheets

Teacher Note: Use after Quick Check page 224 to reteach Unit 8, Lesson 5. (4)

125

Round **8.45** to the nearest whole number. The nearest whole number to **8.45** is either **8** or **9**.

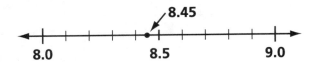

Think: Since **4** tenths is less than **5** tenths, **8.45** is to the left of **8.5** on the number line.

Since **8.45** is closer to **8** than to **9**, **8.45** rounds to **8**.

Round **3.69** to the nearest tenth. The nearest tenth to **3.69** is either **3.6** or **3.7**.

Think: Since **9** hundredths is greater than **5** hundredths, **3.69** is to the right of **3.65** on the number line.

Since **3.69** is closer to **3.7** than to **3.6**, **3.69** rounds to **3.7**.

Write the two whole numbers that the decimal is between.

1. 58.4 is between _____ and _____.

2. 91.72 is between _____ and _____.

3. 23.5 is between _____ and _____.

4. 15.09 is between _____ and _____.

Underline the ones digit. Circle the tenths digit. Round the decimal to the nearest whole number.

5. 23.9 _____

6. 84.03 _____

7. 16.75 _____

8. 7.2 _____

9. 186.7 _____

10. 218.48 _____

11. 79.09 _____

12. 455.9 _____

Underline the tenths digit. Circle the hundredths digit. Round the decimal to the nearest tenth.

13. 23.94 _____

14. 84.03 _____

15. 16.75 _____

16. 0.28 _____

17. 186.76 _____

18. 218.48 _____

19. 79.09 _____

20. 455.97 _____

Teacher Note: Use after Quick Check page 224 to reteach Unit 8, Lesson 6. **(4)**

When you add with decimals, line up the ones and the decimal points. Add the numbers the same way you add whole numbers. Write the decimal point in your answer.

Add: **4.59 + 3.83**

Ones	.	Tenths	Hundredths
4	.	5	9
3	.	8	3
8	.	4	2

Add: **4.5 + 3.83**

Ones	.	Tenths	Hundredths
4	.	5	
3	.	8	3
8	.	3	3

Find each sum.

1. 7.6 + 1.84

	Ones	.	Tenths	Hundredths
	7	.	6	
+	1	.	8	4

2. 8.5 + 1.32

	Ones	.	Tenths	Hundredths
	8	.	5	
+	1	.	3	2

3. 3.31 + 4.87

	Ones	.	Tenths	Hundredths
	3	.	3	1
+				

4. 5.09 + 2.2

	Ones	.	Tenths	Hundredths
	5	.	0	9
+				

5. 4.96 + 3.19

	Ones	.	Tenths	Hundredths
+				

6. 5.4 + 3.38

	Ones	.	Tenths	Hundredths
+				

7. 2.35 + 4.6 _____

8. 4.08 + 3.22 _____

9. 3.17 + 6.8 _____

Reteach Worksheets

Teacher Note: Use after Quick Check page 228 to reteach Unit 8, Lesson 7. (4)

When you subtract with decimals, line up the ones and the decimal points. Subtract the numbers the same way you subtract whole numbers. Write the decimal point in your answer.

Subtract:

Ones	.	Tenths	Hundredths
4	.	8	6
1	.	4	2
3	.	4	4

Subtract:

Ones	.	Tenths	Hundredths
4	.	5	
3	.	8	3
0	.	6	7

Find each difference.

1. 4.37 − 2.75

Ones	.	Tenths	Hundredths
4	.	3	7
− 2	.	7	5

2. 8.5 − 1.32

Ones	.	Tenths	Hundredths
8	.	5	
− 1	.	3	2

3. 7.24 − 2.18

Ones	.	Tenths	Hundredths
7	.	2	4
−			

4. 3.63 − 2.86

Ones	.	Tenths	Hundredths
3	.	6	3
−			

5. 3.54 − 2.4

Ones	.	Tenths	Hundredths
−			

6. 5.4 − 3.06

Ones	.	Tenths	Hundredths
−			

7. 7 − 4.16 _____

8. 6.09 − 4.5 _____

9. 4.3 − 2.28 _____

Teacher Note: Use after Quick Check page 228 to reteach Unit 8, Lesson 8. (4)

Here is a way to divide **89** by **6.**

Step 1	Step 2	Step 3
Divide tens. Think: $6 \times 10 = 60$ $6 \times 20 = 120$ **120** is too big. $\begin{array}{r} 1 \\ 6\overline{)89} \end{array}$	Multiply and subtract. $\begin{array}{r} 1 \\ 6\overline{)89} \\ -\ 6 \\ \hline 2 \end{array}$	Regroup (bring down next digit). $\begin{array}{r} 1 \\ 6\overline{)89} \\ -\ 6\downarrow \\ \hline 29 \text{ ones} \end{array}$

Step 4	Step 5
Divide ones. Think: $6 \times 4 = 24$ $\begin{array}{r} 14 \\ 6\overline{)89} \\ -\ 6 \\ \hline 29 \end{array}$	Multiply and subtract. $\begin{array}{r} 14R5 \\ 6\overline{)89} \\ -\ 6 \\ \hline 29 \\ -\ 24 \leftarrow 4 \times 6 \\ \hline 5 \\ \uparrow \\ \text{remainder} \end{array}$

Divide.

1. $\begin{array}{r} 37R \\ 5\overline{)187} \\ -\ 15 \\ \hline 37 \\ -\ 35 \\ \hline 2 \end{array}$

2. $\begin{array}{r} 2 \\ 8\overline{)198} \end{array}$

3. $\begin{array}{r} 4 \\ 5\overline{)248} \end{array}$

4. $4\overline{)254}$

5. $3\overline{)233}$

6. $9\overline{)846}$

7. $7\overline{)247}$

8. $8\overline{)493}$

9. $2\overline{)118}$

10. $6\overline{)525}$

11. $8\overline{)368}$

12. $3\overline{)176}$

Teacher Note: Use before unit 9, Lesson 1. **(4)**

Basic multiplication facts and patterns can help you
multiply tens, hundreds, and thousands.

Factors	Product
5 × 8	**40**
5 × 80	**400**
5 × 800	**4,000**
5 × 8,000	**40,000**

3 zeros in   Write **3** zeros
the factors.   at the end of the product.

Follow this rule:
First, use the basic fact. Then write as many
zeros at the end of the product as there are
in both of the factors.

Use the pattern. Complete.

1. 8 × 1 = 8

8 × 10 = 80

8 × 100 = _____

8 × 1,000 = _____

2. 5 × 3 = 15

5 × 30 = _____

5 × 300 = _____

5 × 3,000 = _____

3. 6 × 4 = _____

6 × 40 = _____

6 × 400 = _____

6 × 4,000 = _____

4. 4 × 5 = _____

4 × 50 = _____

4 × 500 = _____

4 × 5,000 = _____

5. 7 × 6 = _____

7 × 60 = _____

7 × 600 = _____

7 × 6,000 = _____

6. 9 × 3 = _____

9 × 30 = _____

9 × 300 = _____

9 × 3,000 = _____

Multiply.

7. 8 × 70 = _____

8. 6 × 500 = _____

9. 2 × 7,000 = _____

10. 7 × 400 = _____

11. 5 × 20 = _____

12. 6 × 80 = _____

13. 8 × 4,000 = _____

14. 6 × 600 = _____

15. 4 × 9,000 = _____

Teacher Note: Use before Unit 9, Lesson 1. **(4)**

The parts of a division sentence are the **divisor,** the **dividend,** and the **quotient.** Sometimes there is a **remainder.**

$$\text{divisor} \rightarrow 18\overline{)64} \leftarrow \text{quotient ?}$$
$$\uparrow$$
$$\text{dividend}$$

Rounding the divisor and the dividend can help you estimate the quotient.

Round **18** to **20** and **64** to **60.**

$$20\overline{)60} \quad 3$$

Now, try your estimate in the original division sentence.

$$18\overline{)64} \quad 3R10$$
$$-54$$
$$10 \leftarrow \text{remainder}$$

Divide.

1. $9\overline{)62}$ Estimate: $10\overline{)60} \quad 6$

Try: $9\overline{)62}$ 6R ___

2. $21\overline{)89}$ Estimate: ___

Try: $21\overline{)89}$

3. $46\overline{)91}$ **4.** $17\overline{)83}$ **5.** $39\overline{)58}$ **6.** $19\overline{)73}$ **7.** $17\overline{)79}$ **8.** $28\overline{)98}$

When you round numbers to estimate the quotients,
your estimate might be too big or too small.

23)‾67‾

23 rounds to **20** and **67** rounds to **70**.

$$\begin{array}{r} 3 \\ 20)\overline{60} \end{array}$$

Try:
$$\begin{array}{r} 3 \\ 23)\overline{67} \\ -69 \end{array}$$

Try again:
$$\begin{array}{r} 2R21 \\ 23)\overline{67} \\ -46 \\ \hline 21 \end{array}$$

69 > 67, so the quotient is too big.

16)‾49‾

16 rounds to **20** and **49** rounds to **50**.

$$\begin{array}{r} 2R10 \\ 20)\overline{50} \end{array}$$

Try:
$$\begin{array}{r} 2 \\ 16)\overline{49} \\ -32 \\ \hline 17 \end{array}$$

Try again:
$$\begin{array}{r} 3R1 \\ 16)\overline{49} \\ -48 \\ \hline 1 \end{array}$$

17 > 16, so the quotient is too small.

**Estimate the quotient. Write *too big* or *too small.*
Then try another estimate.**

1. 19)‾56‾

Estimate

$60 \div 20 = 3$

Try your estimate: Try again:

19)‾56‾   19)‾56‾

too _____

2. 26)‾79‾

Estimate

$80 \div 30 = 2 \ R20$

Try your estimate: Try again:

26)‾79‾   26)‾79‾

too _____

3. 33)‾89‾

Estimate

$90 \div$ _____ = _____

Try your estimate: Try again:

Think: 33)‾89‾   33)‾89‾

too _____

4. 17)‾87‾

Estimate

_____ $\div$ _____ = _____

Try your estimate: Try again:

17)‾87‾   17)‾87‾

too _____

Teacher Note: Use after Quick Check page 242 to reteach Unit 9, Lesson 2. **(4)**

You can round and estimate the quotient for a problem with a three-digit dividend.

For example: Think: **30 × ? = 210**

$29\overline{)214}$

Round the dividend and the divisor to the nearest ten. **29** rounds to **30** and **214** rounds to **210**.

$$\begin{array}{r} 7 \\ 30\overline{)210} \end{array}$$

Now, try your estimate in the original division sentence.

$$\begin{array}{r} \textbf{7R11} \\ 29\overline{)214} \\ -\ 203 \\ \hline 11 \rightarrow \text{remainder} \end{array}$$

Reteach Worksheets

Divide.

1. $92\overline{)569}$ Estimate: $\begin{array}{r} 6 \\ 100\overline{)600} \end{array}$

$$\text{Try: } \begin{array}{r} 6R\text{\_\_\_\_\_} \\ 92\overline{)569} \\ -\ 552 \\ \hline \end{array}$$

2. $21\overline{)193}$ Estimate: $\overline{)}$

Try: $21\overline{)193}$

3. $39\overline{)168}$ Estimate: $\overline{)}$

4. $74\overline{)683}$ Estimate: $\overline{)}$

5. $49\overline{)486}$

6. $67\overline{)163}$

7. $69\overline{)109}$

8. $51\overline{)306}$

You can use rounding and estimation when the quotient is **10** or more.

Divide: $26\overline{)653}$

| Use compatible numbers.

Think: $30 \times ? = 600$
$30 \times 20 = 600$

The quotient must be around **20**. | Try **2** in the tens place.

2
$26\overline{)653}$
$\underline{-\ 52}$
133 | Divide the ones. Write the remainder.

$25R3$
$26\overline{)653}$
$\underline{-\ 52}$
133
$\underline{-\ 130}$
3 |

Divide.

1. $21\overline{)513}$ Estimate: $25\overline{)500}^{\,20}$

2
$21\overline{)513}$
$\underline{-\ 42}$

2. $16\overline{)368}$ Estimate: $16\overline{)370}$

$16\overline{)368}$

3. $49\overline{)586}$ Estimate: $\overline{)}$

4. $37\overline{)894}$ Estimate: $\overline{)}$

5. $42\overline{)634}$ Estimate: _____

6. $28\overline{)896}$ Estimate: _____

Teacher Note: Use after Quick Check page 250 to reteach Unit 9, Lesson 4. **(4)**

Sometimes there will be a zero in the quotient.

Divide: $23\overline{)481}$

Think:
$20 \times ? = 400$
$20 \times 20 = 400$
The quotient must be around **20**.

Try **2** in the tens place.

$20 \times 23 = 460$

$$\begin{array}{r} 2 \\ 23\overline{)481} \\ -460 \\ \hline 21 \end{array}$$

Think: **21** is less than **23**. Write a **0** in the quotient. The remainder will be **21**.

$$\begin{array}{r} 20R21 \\ 23\overline{)481} \\ -460 \\ \hline 21 \end{array}$$

Divide.

1. $42\overline{)426}$ Estimate: $42\overline{)420}^{\ 10}$

   Try: $\begin{array}{r} 42\overline{)426} \\ -42 \end{array}$

2. $47\overline{)953}$ Estimate: $50\overline{)950}$

   Try: $47\overline{)953}$

3. $19\overline{)583}$ Estimate: _____

4. $16\overline{)333}$ Estimate: _____

5. $49\overline{)517}$ Estimate: _____

6. $37\overline{)765}$ Estimate: _____

Teacher Note: Use after Quick Check page 250 to reteach Unit 9, Lesson 5. (4)

Name _____

Use what you know about long division to solve problems with **4**-digit dividends.

Divide: **1,192 ÷ 29**

Step 1

29)‾1,192

Think:
30 × ? = 1,200
3 × 4 = 12

So, **30 × 40 = 1,200**

Step 2

Try **40** in the original division problem.

4 × 29 = 116

So, **40 × 29 = 1,160**

```
        40
29)‾1,192
  − 1,160
```

Step 3

Solve the whole division problem.

```
        41R3
29)‾1,192
  − 1,160
       32
     − 29
        3
```

Divide.

1. 42)‾1,798   Estimate:

Try:
```
        40
40)‾1,600
```

```
        4
42)‾1,798
  − 168
    118
```

2. 21)‾1,315   Estimate:

Try:
)‾‾‾

21)‾1,315

3. 35)‾2,062   Estimate:
)‾‾‾

4. 19)‾1,372   Estimate:
)‾‾‾

5. 49)‾1,182

6. 37)‾1,198

Teacher Note: Use after Quick Check page 250 to reteach Unit 9, Lesson 7. **(4)**

You can use compatible numbers to estimate quotients in a division problem.

Compatible numbers are numbers that you can divide easily by using division facts. Choose numbers that are close to the numbers in the division sentence.

Estimate **374 ÷ 6**. Then find the exact quotient.

Think: Change the dividend to a compatible number that is a product of the divisor.

Estimate.

$6 \times 60 = 360$

$6 \times 70 = 420$

420 is too big.

374 ÷ 6 is about **60**.

Try **6** in the tens place and complete the problem.

```
    62R2
6)374
  − 36
    14
  − 12
     2
```

Divide.

1. 42)1,694   Choose numbers:
$40 \times 40 = 1,600$
$40 \times 50 = 2,000$

```
       40
42)1,694
  − 168
     14
```

2. 25)1,315   Choose numbers:
$25 \times 40 = 1,000$
$25 \times 50 = 1,250$

```
       52
25)1,315
  − 125
     65
      ?
```

3. 36)144   Compatible numbers:

_____ × _____ = _____

4. 19)1,472   Compatible numbers:

_____ × _____ = _____

5. 49)1,582   Compatible numbers:

_____ × _____ = _____

6. 64)198   Compatible numbers:

_____ × _____ = _____

Name _____

Use a bar graph to compare data.

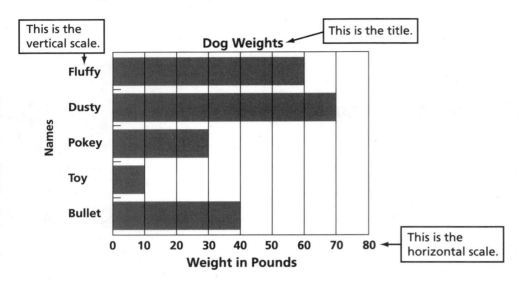

This is the vertical scale.

This is the title.

Dog Weights

Names

Fluffy
Dusty
Pokey
Toy
Bullet

0 10 20 30 40 50 60 70 80

Weight in Pounds

This is the horizontal scale.

1. What does this bar graph show? Look at the title

to find out. _____

2. What do the numbers on the horizontal scale show?

Look at the scale label. _____

3. How much does Bullet weigh? Find the bar for Bullet.
The end of the bar lines up with a number on the
horizontal scale. That number is Bullet's weight.

_____

4. How much does the heaviest dog weigh? Look for

the longest bar. _____

5. These are the dogs' heights:
Fluffy: **24** in., Dusty: **27** in.,
Pokey: **18** in., Toy: **9** in.,
Bullet: **21** in. Draw bars to
finish the graph of the heights.

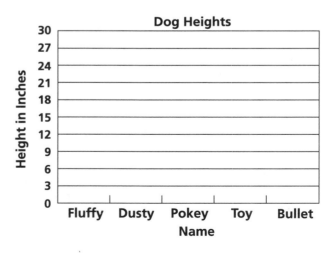

Dog Heights

Height in Inches

30
27
24
21
18
15
12
9
6
3
0

Fluffy Dusty Pokey Toy Bullet

Name

Teacher Note: Use before Unit 10, Lesson 1. **(4)**

You can organize the data in the table by writing each person's name above the number of goals he or she scored.

Number of Goals	
Will	3
Tess	1
Krista	5
Sam	2
Ben	0
Juan	4
Paula	5
Marta	7
Leslie	0
Tia	2
Sara	1
Roy	3
Amy	3
Tony	5
Eric	1
Cole	3

You can also write X's instead of names. This is a **line plot.**

Use the line plot to answer questions 1 and 2.

1. How many people scored **1** goal? Count the number of X's above the **1.** _____

2. How many people scored more than **3** goals? Count the number of X's above **4, 5, 6,** and **7** goals.

_____

Use the table.

3. Write X's above numbers on the line plot to show the data in the table.

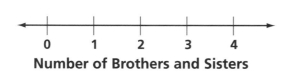

Numbers of Brothers and Sisters			
Gen	2	Mike	1
Lee	0	Vic	4
Emmy	1	Sal	3
Nick	0	Ken	2
Liz	0	Art	2
Alan	3	Pat	2

Reteach Worksheets

Teacher Note: Use before Unit 10, Lesson 1. **(4)**

Name _____

A pictograph uses pictures to show data.

Telephone Calls Made Last Week

Wendy

Ian

Janet

Leroy

Nick

Key: Each 📞 = 5 calls

Use the pictograph to answer these questions.

1. What does this pictograph show? Look at the title.

_____

2. What does each telephone symbol stand for? The key below the graph will tell you.

_____

3. Which three people made the same number of telephone calls? Look for three names that have the same number of symbols after them.

_____

4. Who made the fewest calls? Look for the name with the fewest symbols after it.

_____

5. How many telephone calls did Janet make last week? Count by fives to find out.

_____

6. Who made **25** telephone calls? _____

7. Sara made **15** telephone calls last week. Show what you would write to add this information to

the pictograph. _____

_____

140   **Teacher Note:** Use before Unit 10, Lesson 1. (4)

A circle graph helps you see how the parts of a whole are related.

This circle graph shows the answers to a survey question: What is your favorite bug?

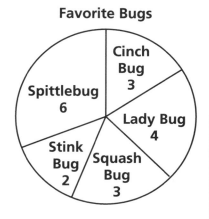

Favorite Bugs

Reteach Worksheets

Use the circle graph to answer the question.

1. Which bug was chosen by the most people? Look at the label for the biggest section.

_____

2. How many people liked the stink bug best? Find stink bug on the graph. Read the number.

_____

3. Which two bugs got the same number of votes? Look for two sections that are the same size.

_____

4. How many people were surveyed? Add the number of votes for all of the bugs.

_____

5. What fraction of the people surveyed voted for spittlebug as their favorite bug? Use the number of votes for the spittlebug as the numerator and the total number of votes as the denominator.

Write the fraction in simplest form. _____

6. Which bug got $\frac{1}{9}$ of the votes? _____

7. Did the squash bug get more than $\frac{1}{4}$ of the votes or less than $\frac{1}{4}$ of the votes? _____

8. Which two bugs each got $\frac{1}{6}$ of the votes?

_____

Teacher Note: Use before Unit 10, Lesson 1. **(4)**

Rosa made a table to gather data for her survey.

HOW MANY MILES FROM SCHOOL DO YOU LIVE?

DISTANCE IN MILES		
MILES	TALLY	TOTAL
LESS THAN 1 |卌 |||	
1 – 5	卌 卌		
6 – 10	卌 ||	
11 – 15	||||	
MORE THAN 15	||	

1. Complete the table. Count the tally marks to find the total number of people who live each distance from school.

2. How many people did Rosa survey? Add the totals to find out. _____

3. Complete the statement: _____ people live between **11** miles and **15** miles from school.

4. How many people live less than **1** mile from school?

_____

5. Do more people live **1–5** miles from school or **6–10** miles from school? How many more?

_____

6. How many people live more than **10** miles from school? _____

7. Write another fact you can learn from the survey.

_____

_____

Teacher Note: Use after Quick Check page 270 to reteach Unit 10, Lesson 1. **(4)**

The table shows the number of hours each person slept last night.

Name	Hours Slept
Alexio	8
Vailea	7
Marta	9
Eva	8
Neil	8
Mike	9
Leslie	7
Keith	4
Louis	8
Alana	9
Amelia	7
Carey	10
Austin	8
Rosa	9
Aldo	8

1. Complete the line plot to show the data in the table. For each person, put an *X* above the number of hours he or she slept.

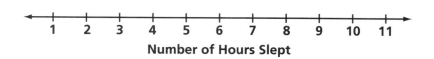

Number of Hours Slept

Use your line plot to answer these questions.

2. What is the mode? The mode is the number that occurs most frequently. Look for the number with the most *X*'s above it. _____

3. What is the range? Subtract the fewest hours slept from the most hours slept. The difference is the range. _____

4. Does this set of data have an outlier? If so, what number is the outlier? Look for a number that is far apart from the other numbers in the data set.

_____

5. What is the median number of hours slept? Use the line plot to write the numbers in order. The median is the middle number. _____

Add these times to the line plot: Jason, 9 hours; Tammy, 9 hours; Paula, 9 hours. Then use the line plot.

6. What are the new mode, median, and range?

_____

Scott planted a seed. He measures the height of the plant once a week and graphs the plant's growth.

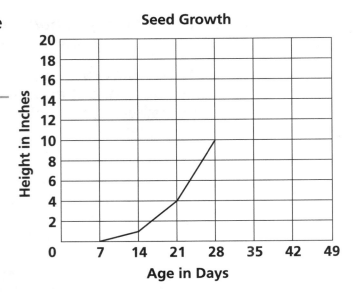

Seed Growth

Use the graph to answer these questions.

1. What does the horizontal scale show? Look at the bottom of

   the graph. _____

2. What does the vertical scale show? Look at the left side

   of the graph. _____

3. At what age was the plant **4** inches tall? Find **4** inches on the vertical scale. Then follow the grid line across to the point where the graph crosses **4** inches. Follow the other grid line down from the

   point and read the age. _____

4. Between what two ages did the plant grow the most? The steepest part of the line shows the

   greatest growth. _____

5. Between **14** and **28** days of age, how many inches did the plant grow? Read the plant's height at age **14** days and at age **28** days from the graph.

   _____

6. Would you expect the plant's height to increase, decrease, or remain the same between age **28** days and age **35** days? Explain.

   _____

7. Graph the next three measurements.

Age	Height
35 days	**14** inches
42 days	**16** inches
49 days	**18** inches

Teacher Note: Use after Quick Check page 270 to reteach Unit 10, Lesson 4. **(4)**

Use the colored balls shown to answer the questions.

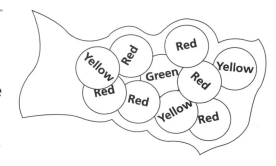

1. What outcomes are possible when taking one ball from the bag? The three colors are the possible outcomes.

   _____

2. Which color are you least likely to get when you pick a ball from the bag?

   _____

3. Complete: _____ out of _____ balls are yellow.

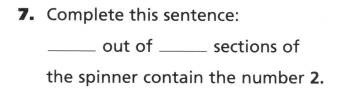

   Number of balls   Total number of balls

4. Complete this sentence: _____ out of _____ balls are red.

5. If you put the ball back and then reach in a second time and take a ball from the bag, what color do you predict it will be? Why?

   _____

Use the spinner for exercises 6–8.

6. If you spin the spinner, what are the possible outcomes? _____

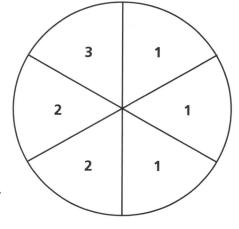

7. Complete this sentence:

   _____ out of _____ sections of the spinner contain the number **2**.

8. Predict which number you will be most likely to land on if you spin the spinner. _____

Teacher Note: Use after Quick Check page 276 to reteach Unit 10, Lesson 5. (4)

Kenneth has **9** marbles in his bag. For the following exercises, suppose Kenneth takes one marble out of the bag.

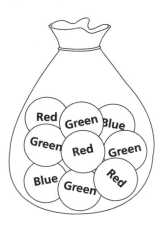

1. Write the number of blue marbles to complete this sentence: The chance that Kenneth will get a

   blue marble is _____ out of **9**.

2. What are the possible outcomes? List the colors of

   the marbles. _____

3. Which outcome is most likely? Look for the color

   of the greatest number of marbles. _____

4. What fraction shows the probability, or chance, that Kenneth will get a green marble? Write the number of green marbles as the numerator and the total number of marbles as the denominator.

   _____

5. What is the probability that Kenneth will get a green marble or a blue marble? Use the sum of the blue and green marbles as the numerator.

   _____

6. Complete this sentence. The chance that Kenneth

   will get a red marble is _____ out of _____.

7. The fraction that shows the probability that

   Kenneth will get a blue marble is _____.

8. Is Kenneth more likely to get a blue marble or a

   red marble? _____

9. What is the probability that Kenneth will get a blue marble or a red marble?

   _____

Teacher Note: Use after Quick Check page 276 to reteach Unit 10, Lesson 6. **(4)**

A **tree diagram** is one way to find all of the possible outcomes for an experiment. This tree diagram shows the possible outcomes for flipping a coin and tossing a number cube.

1. What are the possible outcomes for flipping a coin? Write the names for the sides of a coin. _____

2. What are the possible outcomes for tossing a number cube? Write the numbers you can get if you toss the cube.

_____

3. How many possible outcomes are there for flipping a coin and tossing a number cube? Count the number of branches on the tree diagram.

_____ possible outcomes

Coin Flip	Cube Toss
Heads	1 2 3 4 5 6
Tails	1 2 3 4 5 6

Nadia can order a blue or a red sweatshirt in one of four sizes: small, medium, large, or extra-large.

4. What are the color choices?

_____

5. What are the size choices?

_____

6. Draw a tree diagram in the box. Match each color with each size to show all of the different sweatshirts Nadia can order.

7. How many different sweatshirts can Nadia

order? _____

Color	Size

This is how you locate point **(3, 2)** on a grid.

Start at **0.**   Move **3** spaces across.   Move **2** spaces up.

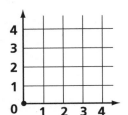 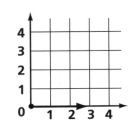 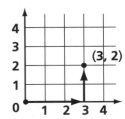

(3, 2) is an ordered pair. The order is (across **3**, up **2**).

Use the grid. Name the letter for the ordered pair.

1. **(1, 3)** _____
Start at **0.**
Go **1** space across.
Go **3** spaces up.

2. **(4, 2)** _____

Start at _____.

Go _____ space across.

Go _____ spaces up.

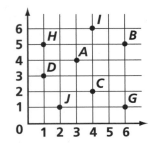

3. **(6, 5)** _____   **4.** **(3, 4)** _____

This is how you find the ordered pair for point *M.*

Locate the point.   Trace down to **2.**   Trace across to **4.**

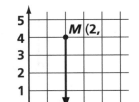 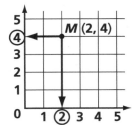

Use the same grid you used for exercises 1–4.
Find the ordered pair for each point.

5. *G* _____   **6.** *H* _____

Trace down to **6.**   Trace down to _____.

Trace across to **1.**   Trace across to _____.

Teacher Note: Use before Unit 11, Lesson 1. **(4)**

● An **algebraic expression** is a short way to write a word phrase.

This is a word phrase: Subtract five from your age.

This is an arithmetic expression: $\square - 5$

This is an algebraic expression: $a - 5$

The letter *a* is a **variable.** It stands for "your age." Just as people's ages vary, *a* varies.

Write an algebraic expression for the word phrase.

1. the product of **7** and your dog's age

     Choose a letter for the variable. _____

     Choose an operation symbol. _____

     Write the expression. _____

● **2.** **9** added to the number of baseball cards

     _____

3. **2** more than the number of children

     _____

Match each word phrase with an algebraic expression.

4. _____ divide the number of hours by **3**   a. $5 + c$

5. _____ the number of windows multiplied by **8**   b. $h + 2$

6. _____ **8** less than the number of tickets   c. $h \div 3$

7. _____ the number of cats added to **5**   d. $2 \times b$

8. _____ **2** more than the number of hats   e. $8 \times w$

9. _____ the number of shoes divided by **2**   f. $t - 8$

● **10.** _____ double the number of blankets   g. $4 \times c$

11. _____ **4** times the number of cars   h. $s \div 2$

Teacher Note: Use after Quick Check page 290 to reteach Unit 11, Lesson 1. **(4)**

This is an **equation.** The values on both sides of the equal sign are the same.

♦♦♦♦♦   ♦♦   ♦♦♦♦♦♦♦

5   +   2   =   7

Both sides of this equation are equal to **7.**

If you add the same number to both sides of an equation, the values on both sides of the equal sign are still the same.

♦♦♦♦♦   ♦♦   ♦   ♦♦♦♦♦♦♦   ♦

5   +   2   +   1   =   7   +   1

Both sides of this equation are equal to **8.**

If you multiply both sides of an equation by the same number, the values on both sides of the equation are still the same.

♦♦♦♦♦   ♦♦   ♦♦♦♦♦♦♦
♦♦♦♦♦   ♦♦   ♦♦♦♦♦♦♦

(5   +   2)   x   2   =   7   x   2

Both sides of this equation are equal to **14.**

Complete each equation.

1. $2 + 3 + 4 = 5 +$ _____

$9 = 5 +$ _____

2. $6 \times 3 = (4 + 2) \times$ _____

$18 = 6 \times$ _____

3. $1 + 6 + 2 =$ _____ $+ 2$

$9 = 7 +$ _____

4. $(1 + 5) \times 2 =$ _____ $\times 2$

$6 \times 2 =$ _____ $\times 2$

5. $4 + 5 = 3 + 1 +$ _____

6. _____ $\times 3 = (6 + 2) \times 3$

7. $9 + 4 +$ _____ $= 13 + 2$

8. $7 \times 5 = (2 + 5) \times$ _____

Teacher Note: Use after Quick Check page 290 to reteach Unit 11, Lesson 2. **(4)**

An equation is a short way to write a mathematical sentence.

Sentence:　The price of the shirt plus **$2** tax is **$34**.

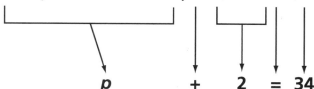

Equation:　　　　　p　　　　$+$　　2　$=$　34

The letter p is a **variable**.
A variable is a letter that stands for an unknown number.

Write an equation for the sentence.

1. The number of people in the theater minus the **15** employees is **82**.

Identify the variable. _____

Choose a letter for the variable. _____

Choose an operation and write an expression. _____

Write = for "is" and complete the equation. _____

2. The number of apples divided by **6** is **8**.

Choose a letter for the variable and an operation.

Write an expression. _____

Write = for "is" and complete the equation. _____

3. Twelve more than the number of boys is **29**. _____

4. The number of boxes times **10** is **120**. _____

5. Eight less than the number of kittens is **9**. _____

6. Forty-five divided by the number of players on the team is **5**. _____

7. The number of cans added to **33** is **91**. _____

Reteach Worksheets

This table shows a pattern. The rule that describes the pattern is: The number of packages times **4** equals the number of lightbulbs.

The equation for this rule is: $p \times 4 = l$.

Find the number of lightbulbs in **4** packages.

Rule: $p \times 4 = l$
Substitute: $p = 4$
                  $4 \times 4 = l$
                  $16 = l$ There are **16** lightbulbs in **4** packages.

Packages (p)	Lightbulbs (l)
1	4
2	8
3	12
4	

Describe the rule. Write an equation. Complete the table.

1.

Members (m)	Total (t)
1	9
2	10
3	11
4	

Rule: The number of members

plus _____ equals the total.

Equation: $m +$ _____ $= t$

2.

Earnings (e)	Profit (p)
$8	$1
$10	$3
$12	$5
$14	$

Rule: The earnings less _____

equals _____.

Equation: $e -$ _____ $=$ _____

3.

Teams (t)	Players (p)
1	11
2	22
3	33
4	

Rule: The number of teams times

_____ equals the number of players.

Equation: _____

4.

Singles (s)	Pairs (p)
4	2
6	3
8	4
10	

Rule: _____

_____.

Equation: _____

Teacher Note: Use after Quick Check page 296 to reteach Unit 11, Lesson 5. **(4)**

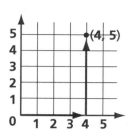

A point on a grid is named by an
ordered pair of numbers.

Locate point **(4, 5)** by starting at zero and moving
4 units to the right, then **5** units up.

Write the letter of the point at each location.

1. **(2, 4)**
Start at **0**.
Move **2** units right.
Move **4** units up.

Read the letter. _____

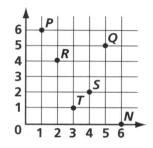

2. **(3, 1)**

Start at _____.

Move _____ units right.

Move _____ unit up.

Read the letter. _____

3. **(1, 6)** _____   **4.** **(5, 5)** _____   **5.** **(4, 2)** _____

Write the ordered pair for each point.

6. *U*
From **0**, point *U* is **0** units right
and **5** units up.

The ordered pair is _____.

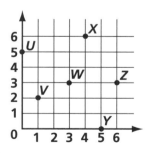

7. *V*

From **0**, point *V* is _____ unit

right and _____ units up.

The ordered pair is _____.

8. *W* _____   **9.** *X* _____   **10.** *Y* _____

Teacher Note: Use after Quick Check page 296 to reteach Unit 11, Lesson 6. **(4)**   **153**

In an ordered pair **(x, y)**, *x* gives the horizontal location and *y* gives the vertical location of the point.

Here is one way to find the location for an ordered pair such as **(4, 6)**.

Locate **4** on the *x*-axis.

Locate **6** on the *y*-axis.

Follow the lines.

Locate the point **(4, 6)**.

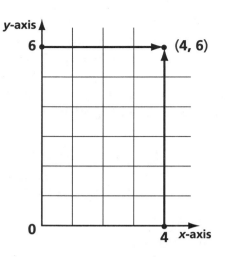

Locate and label the point on the grid.

1. *D* (1, 5)
   Locate **1** on the *x*-axis.
   Locate **5** on the *y*-axis.
   Locate point **(1, 5)**.

2. *E* (5, 5)

   Locate _____ on the *x*-axis.

   Locate _____ on the *y*-axis.

3. *F* (5, 8)   **4.** *G* (1, 8)

5. Connect the points in alphabetical order.

   Name the figure. _____

6. *Q* (0, 1)   **7.** *R* (2, 2)   **8.** *S* (4, 3)   **9.** *T* (8, 5)

10. Connect the points for exercises **6–9**. Name the figure. _____

11. *L* (4, 0)   **12.** *M* (8, 0)   **13.** *N* (8, 2)

14. Connect the points for exercises **11–13**. Name the figure. _____

Teacher Note: Use after Quick Check page 302 to reteach Unit 11, Lesson 7. **(4)**

You can use a rule to find ordered pairs.

| Substitute a value for *x* into the rule.

Rule: $x \div 2 = y$
Let $x = 2$ | Solve for *y*.

$2 \div 2 = y$
$1 = y$ | Write the ordered pair (x, y).

$x = 2, y = 1$
(2, 1) |

1. Complete the table. Find ordered pairs for the rule $x \div 2$.

x	x ÷ 2	y	Ordered Pair (x, y)
2	2 ÷ 2	1	(2, 1)
4	4 ÷ 2		
6	6 ÷ 2		
8	8 ÷ 2		
10	10 ÷ 2		

Rule $x \div 2$

Let $x = 4, y = 4 \div 2$

$y =$ _____

Ordered pair: (4, _____)

Let $x = 6, y = 6 \div 2$

$y =$ _____

Ordered pair: (_____)

2. Complete the table. Find ordered pairs for the rule $x + 3$.

x	x + 3	y	Ordered Pair (x, y)
0	0 + 3	3	(0, 3)
1	1 + 3		
2	2 + 3		
3			
4			

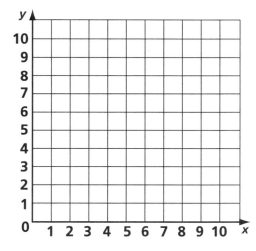

3. Graph the ordered pairs for the rule $x \div 2$. Connect the points in order. Name the figure.

_____

4. Graph the ordered pairs for the rule $x + 3$. Connect the points in order. Name the figure.

_____

Teacher Note: Use after Quick Check page 302 to reteach Unit 11, Lesson 8. **(4)**

Extension Worksheets

Extension Worksheets

NOTES

You can use logical reasoning to help you decide if statements are true or false. The diagram shows figures of different sizes and shapes. The circles can help you decide if the statements are true or false.

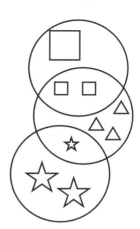

Statements:

- All of the stars are small.
  False, because 2 of the stars are large.

- Some of the squares are large.
  True, because 1 square is large.

- None of the large figures are triangles.
  True, because the large figures are either squares or stars.

Use the above diagram for statements 1–4.
Write *true* or *false* for each statement.

1. All of the triangles are small.

_____

2. All of the squares are small.

_____

3. None of the stars are large.

_____

4. Some of the small figures are squares.

_____

Use the diagram at the right for statements 5–9.
If the statement is true, write *true*. If the statement is false, rewrite the statement to make it true.

5. Some of the squares have stripes.

_____

6. None of the diamonds are plain.

_____

7. All of the figures with stripes are triangles.

_____

8. None of the dotted figures are triangles.

_____

9. All of the triangles are plain.

_____

Teacher Note: Use after Unit 1, Lesson 4. **(4)**

The Romans used letters and combinations of letters as the symbols for numbers.

Standard Numerals	1	5	10	50	100	500	1,000
Roman Numerals	I	V	X	L	C	D	M

Here are the Roman numerals for **1** to **10**:

I	II	III	IV	V	VI	VII	VIII	IX	X
1	**2**	**3**	**4**	**5**	**6**	**7**	**8**	**9**	**10**

Rules for reading and writing Roman numerals:

1. Add the value when the symbols repeat.	II is **1 + 1 = 2** CC is **100 + 100 = 200**
2. Add the value when a symbol of lesser value is to the right.	VI is **5 + 1 = 6** LX is **50 + 10 = 60**
3. Subtract the value when a symbol of lesser value is to the left.	IV is **5 − 1 = 4** XC is **100 − 10 = 90**
4. Never repeat the same symbol more than **3** times.	For **400**, write CD, not CCCC.

It can take many symbols to write greater numbers.
The year 1987 is written MCMLXXXVII:
1,000 + (1,000–100) + 50 + 10 + 10 + 10 + 5 + 1 + 1

Show the additions and subtractions to find the values.

1. III _____

2. VII _____

3. IX _____

4. XXII _____

5. XL _____

6. LXX _____

7. LI _____

8. LXII _____

9. DC _____

10. XCV _____

11. LXXV _____

12. CXL _____

Write the Roman numeral.

13. 17 _____

14. 45 _____

15. 54 _____

16. 81 _____

17. 102 _____

18. 1,500 _____

19. 250 _____

20. 1,600 _____

Teacher Note: Use after Unit 1, Lesson 5. **(4)**

Name _____

Break apart numbers to add or subtract mentally.

1. Use breaking apart numbers to make multiples of ten.

Find **58 + 5.**		Find **73 − 8.**	
Break apart **5.**	**58 + 5**	Break apart **8.**	**73 − 8**
Use the Associative Property to make a multiple of **10.**	**(58 + 2) + 3** **60 + 3 = 63**	Use the Associative Property to make a multiple of **10.**	**(73 − 3) − 5** **70 − 5 = 65**

2. Break apart numbers to add or subtract from left to right.

Find **162 + 235.**

Add hundreds.	Add tens.	Add ones.	
100	60	2	
+ 200	+ 30	+ 5	
300	90	7	**300 + 90 + 7 = 397**

Find **5,728 − 1,412.**

Subtract thousands.	Subtract hundreds.	Subtract tens.	Subtract ones.	
5,000	700	20	8	
− 1,000	− 400	− 10	− 2	
4,000	300	10	6	**4,000 + 300 + 10 + 6 = 4,316**

Solve. Use breaking apart numbers.

1. 19 + 7 _____ **2.** 28 + 7 _____ **3.** 56 + 8 _____

4. 52 − 6 _____ **5.** 81 − 5 _____ **6.** 33 − 8 _____

7. 68 + 5 _____ **8.** 85 + 9 _____ **9.** 79 + 9 _____

10. 44 − 5 _____ **11.** 22 − 7 _____ **12.** 61 − 3 _____

13. 734 + 404 _____ **14.** 715 + 183 _____ **15.** 272 + 413 _____

16. 538 − 205 _____ **17.** 247 − 115 _____ **18.** 582 − 340 _____

19. 5,162 + 1,423 _____ **20.** 7,014 + 324 _____

21. 2,659 − 1,637 _____ **22.** 4,879 − 2,750 _____

Extension Worksheets

You can make a triangular pattern of numbers called **Pascal's triangle.** Each row begins and ends with **1.** Each other number is the sum of the two numbers above it.

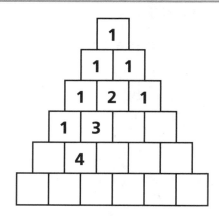

1. Use the pattern described above to complete the triangle.

2. Which two numbers in row **4** produce the **6** in row **5?** _____

3. How did you get the fives in row **6?** _____

4. What will be the numbers in row **7?** _____

5. What will be the numbers in row **8?** _____

6. Write the sum of the numbers in each row.

   What pattern do you notice? _____

   _____

7. Describe another pattern you notice in Pascal's triangle.

   _____

   _____

   _____

You can use array diagrams to multiply 2-digit numbers.
Use an array diagram to find **42 × 35.**

1. Multiply the tens.

2. Multiply the tens and ones.

3. Multiply the ones.

	30	5
40	40 × 30 = 1,200	40 × 5 = 200
2	2 × 30 = 60	2 × 5 = 10

4. Add the four products to find the final product.
   1,200 + 200 + 60 + 10 = 1,470

Complete the array diagram. Then add to find the product.

1. 37
     × 24

	30	7
20	20 × 30 =	20 × 7 =
4	4 × 30 =	4 × 7 =

_____ + _____ + _____ + _____ = _____

2. 42
     × 59

	40	2
50		
9		

_____ + _____ + _____ + _____ = _____

3. 48
     × 84

	40	8
80		
4		

_____ + _____ + _____ + _____ = _____

Complete the array diagram. Then write the two factors and the product.

4.

	_____	3
40	40 × 20 = 800	
_____		6 × 3 = 18

_____ × _____ = _____

5.

	50	_____
_____		20 × 7 =
3	3 × 50 = 150	

_____ × _____ = _____

Name _____

You know that the order of operations can help you simplify expressions. These rules are like having the key to a secret code. They can help you "break the code" to tell the meaning of any expression.

$(3 + 8) \times 2$ This means: *the sum of 3 and 8, multiplied by 2*, or **22**

$3 + (8 \times 2)$ But this means: *the product of 8 and 2, added to 3*, or **19**

Then, $(3 + 8) \times 2 > 3 + (8 \times 2)$.

Use the order of operations. Write the meaning of each expression in words.

1. $9 - (3 \times 2)$ _____

$(9 - 3) \times 2$ _____

2. $(24 \div 6) - 3$ _____

$24 \div (6 - 3)$ _____

3. $(18 + 2) \times (5 - 4)$ _____

Write each expression. Remember to use parentheses when you need to.

4. eight less than the product of eight and four

_____

5. seventy-two divided by the difference between twenty-eight and sixteen

_____

6. the sum of twenty-one and nine, multiplied by three

_____

7. the difference of sixteen and eight, multiplied by two and added to six

_____

     Teacher Note: Use after Unit 4, Lesson 2. **(4)**

● Any composite number can be shown as the product of factors that are prime numbers.

Use a factor tree to find the **prime factorization** of **24**.

Start by choosing a pair of factors, such as **2** and **12**. The number **2** is a prime number. Find another pair of factors for **12**.

Continue factoring until all the factors are prime numbers.

List the factors in order from least to greatest. The prime factorization of **24** is **2 × 2 × 2 × 3**.

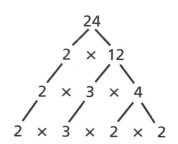

Complete the factor tree. Write the prime factorization.

1.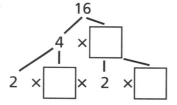

2.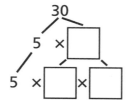

3.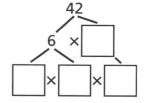

_____   _____   _____

4.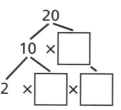

5.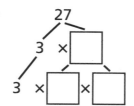

6.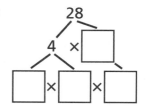

_____   _____   _____

7.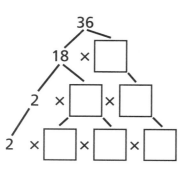

8.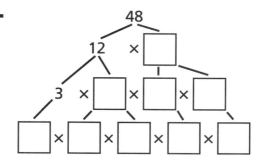

_____   _____

Extension Worksheets

Teacher Note: Use after Unit 4, Lesson 11. **(4)**

Name _____

There are **12** cookies to share equally with **3** people.

If you divide the cookies into **3** equal groups, each group is $\frac{1}{3}$ of **12**.

$\frac{1}{3}$ of 12 = 4 $\frac{2}{3}$ of 12 = 8 $\frac{3}{3}$ of 12 = 12

Solve. Draw a picture if you need to.

1. $\frac{1}{2}$ of 12 = _____   **2.** $\frac{2}{2}$ of 12 = _____   **3.** $\frac{1}{4}$ of 12 = _____

4. $\frac{2}{4}$ of 12 = _____   **5.** $\frac{3}{4}$ of 12 = _____   **6.** $\frac{4}{4}$ of 12 = _____

7. $\frac{1}{6}$ of 12 = _____   **8.** $\frac{2}{6}$ of 12 = _____   **9.** $\frac{4}{6}$ of 12 = _____

You can also use division and multiplication.

$\frac{1}{4}$ of 20 = 20 ÷ 4 = 5

So $\frac{1}{4}$ of 20 = **5**.

If you have more than **1** part of a fraction, you first find the number for **1** part.
Then you multiply to find the number for all parts.

$\frac{3}{4}$ of 16 = ? > First find $\frac{1}{4}$ of **16**.

16 ÷ 4 = 4 > Then multiply to find the number for **3** parts.

3 × 4 = 12

So $\frac{3}{4}$ of 16 = **12**.

Solve.

10. $\frac{1}{6}$ of 18 = ?

18 ÷ 6 = _____

So $\frac{1}{6}$ of 18 = _____

11. $\frac{4}{6}$ of 18 = ?

18 ÷ 6 = _____

_____ × 4 = _____

So $\frac{4}{6}$ of 18 = _____

Teacher Note: Use after Unit 5, Lesson 2. **(4)**

A **flip** is a move that makes the figure face in the opposite direction. Flips are also called **reflections**.

Triangle *B* is a flip image of Triangle *A*.

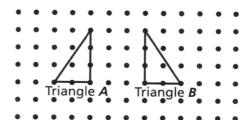

A **slide** is a move in which every point of the figure moves the same distance and same direction.

Trapezoid *D* is the slide image of Trapezoid *C*.

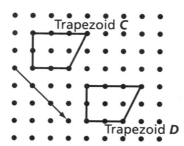

Circle the pairs of figures that are flips. Underline the pairs of figures that are slides.

1.

2.

3.

4.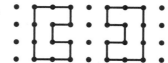

Continue the pattern by drawing four more flip images.

5.

Draw a slide image for the figure.

6.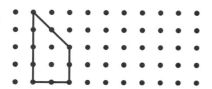

7.

Extension Worksheets

Teacher Note: Use after Unit 6, Lesson 7. **(4)**

Figures that have the same shape are called **similar figures.** Similar figures do not have to be the same size.

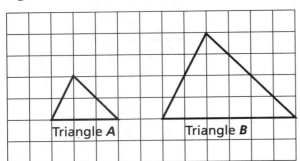

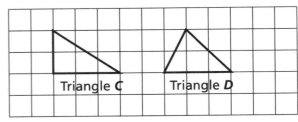

Triangles *A* and *B* are similar figures.

Triangles *C* and *D* are not similar figures.

Write *similar* or *not similar* for the pair of figures.

1.

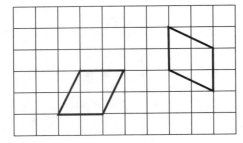

_____

2.

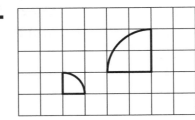

_____

3.

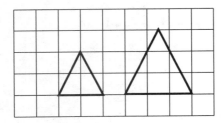

_____

4.

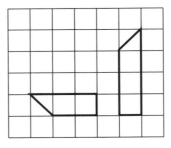

_____

Draw three figures similar to the one shown.

5.

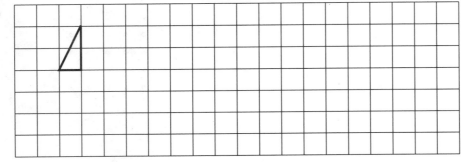

Teacher Note: Use after Unit 6, Lesson 8. **(4)**

Name _____

Making Generalizations

	Picture	Definition
square		A polygon having **4** right angles and **4** congruent sides
rectangle		A polygon having **4** right angles and **4** sides
parallelogram		A quadrilateral in which both pairs of opposite sides are parallel
rhombus (plural: **rhombi**)		A quadrilateral with **4** congruent sides
trapezoid		A quadrilateral with exactly **1** pair of parallel sides

Use the information in the chart to decide whether each statement is true or false. Explain your decision.

1. All squares are rectangles. _____

_____

2. All rectangles are squares. _____

_____

3. All rhombi are parallelograms. _____

_____

4. All parallelograms are rectangles. _____

_____

5. No trapezoids are parallelograms. _____

_____

6. Some rhombi are squares. _____

_____

Copyright © Houghton Mifflin Company. All rights reserved.

Teacher Note: Use after Unit 6, Lesson 9. **(4)**

169

Name _____

There are six time zones in the United States.

Hawaii	Alaska	Pacific	Mountain	Central	Eastern
5:00 A.M.	**6:00** A.M.	**7:00** A.M.	**8:00** A.M.	**9:00** A.M.	**10:00** A.M.

Hawaii Time Zone   Alaska Time Zone   Pacific Time Zone   Mountain Time Zone   Central Time Zone   Eastern Time Zone

Moving from east to west, it is **1** hour earlier in each new time zone.

Write the time for the city when it is 12:00 noon in Tulsa, Oklahoma.

CITY	TIME
Tulsa, Oklahoma, (OK)	**12:00** Noon
1. Los Angeles, California, (CA)	_____
2. Birmingham, Alabama, (AL)	_____
3. Honolulu, Hawaii, (HI)	_____
4. Chicago, Illinois, (IL)	_____
5. Denver, Colorado, (CO)	_____
6. Phoenix, Arizona, (AZ)	_____
7. Juneau, Alaska, (AK)	_____
8. Reno, Nevada, (NV)	_____
9. New York, New York, (NY)	_____
10. Little Rock, Arkansas, (AR)	_____

170

Teacher Note: Use after Unit 7, Lesson 7. **(4)**

The map below is a **scale drawing**. It uses a short distance to stand for a longer real distance. The distance from Ann's house to school measures **7** cm on the map. The scale shows that **1** cm stands for **1** km of real distance, so Ann's house is really **7** km from school.

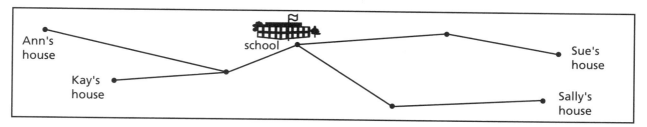

Scale: **1** cm stands for **1** km.

Use a cm ruler. Complete the table.

		Map Distance	Real Distance
1.	from Kay's house to school		
2.	from Sue's house to school		
3.	from Sally's house to school		

Use the map below to complete exercises 4–10.

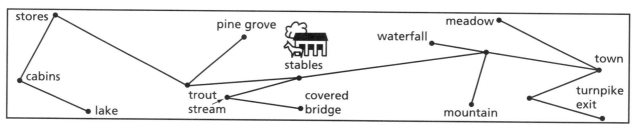

Scale: **1** cm stands for **2** km.

		Map Distance	Real Distance
4.	from the cabins to the stores		
5.	from the turnpike exit to the town		
6.	from the cabins to the pine grove		
7.	from the cabins to the stables		
8.	from the mountain to the waterfall		
9.	from the stores to the covered bridge		
10.	from the lake to the trout stream		

Teacher Note: Use after Unit 7, Lesson 7. **(4)**

171

There are two ways to change a fraction, such as $\frac{13}{20}$, to a decimal.

Method 1
Write an equivalent fraction that has a denominator of **10** or **100**.

Think: The denominator is **20**, so multiply the denominator and the numerator by **5**.

$$\frac{13}{20} = \frac{13 \times 5}{20 \times 5} = \frac{65}{100} = 0.65$$

Method 2
Divide the numerator by the denominator.

$$\frac{13}{20} \rightarrow \begin{array}{r} 0.65 \\ 20\overline{)13.00} \\ -120 \\ \hline 100 \\ -100 \\ \hline 0 \end{array} \leftarrow \text{Write zeros to the right of decimal point.}$$

Complete each statement.

1. Write $\frac{2}{5}$ with a denominator of **10**.

$\frac{2}{5} = \frac{2 \times \square}{5 \times \square} =$ _____. The equivalent decimal for $\frac{2}{5}$

is _____.

2. Write $\frac{9}{20}$ with a denominator of **100**.

$\frac{9}{20} = \frac{9 \times \square}{20 \times \square} =$ _____. The equivalent

decimal for $\frac{9}{20}$ is _____.

Divide to write the fraction as a decimal.

3. $\frac{3}{4} = 4\overline{)3.00}$

4. $\frac{3}{5} = 5\overline{)3.00}$

5. $\frac{8}{25} =$ __$\overline{)}$

Write the fraction as a decimal.

6. $\frac{39}{50} =$ _____

7. $\frac{12}{25} =$ _____

8. $\frac{17}{20} =$ _____

Compare. Use >, <, or =.

9. $\frac{1}{4}$ ◯ 1.25

10. $\frac{3}{4}$ ◯ 0.85

11. $\frac{3}{5}$ ◯ 0.45

Teacher Note: Use after Unit 8, Lesson 5. (4)

Here is a short way to divide by a one-digit number.
You do the division, multiplication, and subtraction in
your head.

Long Division

```
    85
7)597
  56
  ──
   37
   35
   ──
    2
```

Short Division

Think: How many **7**'s in **59**? **8 R3**

Write the quotient **8** and the remainder **3** like this.

```
    8
7)59³7
```

Think: How many **7**'s in **37**? **5 R2**

Write **5** in the quotient and the remainder **2**.

```
  8 5 R2
7)59³7
```

Write only the quotient and any remainder for each problem.

1.
```
 1 5 6 R3
5)7²8³3
```

2. 6)683

3. 4)957

4. 5)876

5. 6)973

6. 3)356

7. 7)725

8. 4)471

9. 5)1,265

10. 6)1,971

11. 8)1,690

12. 7)3,461

Solve each problem in your head and complete the table.

Quotient	10		5		4			4
Divisor	8	8	8	8	8	8	9	9
Dividend		65		58		94	29	
Remainder	2		3		4			3

Extension Worksheets

Teacher Note: Use after Unit 9, Lesson 2. **(4)**

Name _____

You divide a **5**-digit number the same way you divide
any other dividend.

Solve. Study the example.

1. 51)38,762
       760 R2
     357
     306
     306
      02

2. 47)35,642

3. 73)15,895

4. 48)11,906

5. 34)13,765

6. 24)23,971

7. 18)16,459

8. 53)47,456

9. 63)32,454

10. 56)44,856

11. 45)35,567

12. 81)72,366

Teacher Note: Use after Unit 9, Lesson 9. **(4)**

To compare two sets of data, you can show them on the same graph. This **double bar graph** shows zoo attendance for adults and for children.

1. Look at the key. What do the light colored bars show?

   _____

2. On what day did the greatest number of children go to the zoo?

   _____

3. On what day did the number of adults and the number of children differ the most?

   _____

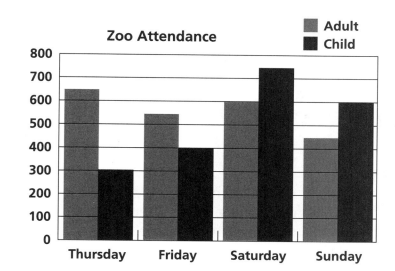

4. Make a double bar graph to show the number of cats and dogs at the animal hospital each day. Remember to label each scale, to provide a key, and to title your graph.

Animal Hospital Patients				
	Fri	Sat	Sun	Mon
Cats	25	30	20	15
Dogs	15	25	20	25

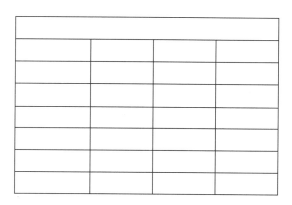

Extension Worksheets

You can use a **double line graph** to show two sets of data. The table shows the number of stuffed animals in two collections.

Use the data in the table to make a double line graph showing the number of stuffed animals Carol and Angela had in their collections each month.

Stuffed Animal Collection		
Month	Carol	Angela
March	1	18
April	2	21
May	5	19
June	7	19
July	10	16
August	12	12
September	16	11
October	20	9

1. Draw dots to show the number of animals in Carol's collection each month. Connect the dots to make a line graph.

2. Use a different color pencil to draw dots to show the number of animals in Angela's collection. Connect the dots to make a line graph.

3. What month did Carol and Angela have the same number of stuffed animals? How do you know?

   _____

   _____

   _____

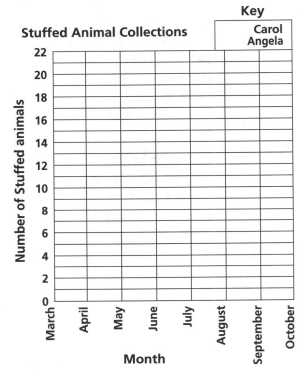

4. In June, who had more stuffed animals? How many more? _____

5. In October, who had more stuffed animals? How many more? _____

6. Compare the change in the number of stuffed animals in each girl's collection. _____

   _____

Teacher Note: Use after Unit 10, Lesson 4. **(4)**

The table shows the ages of the players on a baseball team. To analyze the ages, you can organize them in a stem-and-leaf plot.

Ages of Baseball Players
23, 32, 34, 26, 35, 30, 42, 38, 22, 33, 29, 26, 37, 48, 19, 27, 25, 28, 18, 44, 40, 51

Start by listing the tens digits for the ages as stems. You can then write just the ones digits for the ages. The ones digits are the leaves.

This is a stem-and-leaf plot for the data above.

Stem	Leaves
1	9 8
2	3 6 2 9 6 8 7 5
3	2 4 5 0 8 3 7
4	2 8 4 0
5	1

Use the stem-and-leaf plot above to complete this stem-and-leaf plot. Arrange the leaves following each stem in order from least to greatest.

1.

Stem	Leaves
1	8 9
2	
3	
4	
5	

Use your stem-and-leaf plot to answer these questions.

2. How old is the youngest member of the team?

_____

3. How old is the oldest player? _____

4. There are two players that are the same age.

How old are they? _____

5. Are the most players between **10** and **19** years old, between **20** and **29** years old, between **30** and **39** years old, or older than **39**?

Extension Worksheets

Decreasing | Increasing

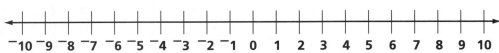

⁻10 ⁻9 ⁻8 ⁻7 ⁻6 ⁻5 ⁻4 ⁻3 ⁻2 ⁻1 0 1 2 3 4 5 6 7 8 9 10

As you move right on the number line, the
numbers increase.
Compare ⁻2 and 6.
Locate ⁻2 on the number line. Then locate 6.
From ⁻2, you move right to 6. ⁻2 is less than 6.

⁻2 < 6

As you move left on the number line, the
numbers decrease.
Compare ⁻3 and ⁻8.
Locate ⁻3 and ⁻8 on the number line.
From ⁻3, you move left to ⁻8. ⁻3 is greater than ⁻8.

⁻3 > ⁻8

**Use the number line above. Compare the
numbers. Write > or <.**

1.	4 ◯ 7	**2.**	⁻5 ◯ ⁻1	**3.**	3 ◯ ⁻2
4.	6 ◯ 0	**5.**	⁻9 ◯ 2	**6.**	⁻3 ◯ 0
7.	⁻8 ◯ ⁻10	**8.**	10 ◯ 3	**9.**	7 ◯ ⁻7
10.	⁻3 ◯ ⁻1	**11.**	⁻4 ◯ ⁻8	**12.**	9 ◯ ⁻2

Write in order from least to greatest.

13. ⁻5, ⁻3, ⁻9 _____   **14.** 4, 0, 9 _____

15. ⁻6, 7, 3 _____   **16.** ⁻5, ⁻10, 5 _____

**Write two numbers that are between each pair
of numbers.**

17. ⁻9, _____, _____, ⁻1   **18.** ⁻4, _____, _____, 4

19. ⁻6, _____, _____, 0   **20.** 6, _____, _____, 9

Teacher Note: Use after Unit 11, Lesson 1. (4)

Teaching Resources

Teaching Resources

Unit ____ Cumulative Review

Mark the space for the answer you have chosen.

1. Ⓐ Ⓑ Ⓒ Ⓓ Ⓔ
2. Ⓕ Ⓖ Ⓗ Ⓙ Ⓚ
3. Ⓐ Ⓑ Ⓒ Ⓓ Ⓔ
4. Ⓕ Ⓖ Ⓗ Ⓙ Ⓚ
5. Ⓐ Ⓑ Ⓒ Ⓓ Ⓔ
6. Ⓕ Ⓖ Ⓗ Ⓙ Ⓚ
7. Ⓐ Ⓑ Ⓒ Ⓓ Ⓔ
8. Ⓕ Ⓖ Ⓗ Ⓙ Ⓚ
9. Ⓐ Ⓑ Ⓒ Ⓓ Ⓔ
10. Ⓕ Ⓖ Ⓗ Ⓙ Ⓚ
11. Ⓐ Ⓑ Ⓒ Ⓓ Ⓔ
12. Ⓕ Ⓖ Ⓗ Ⓙ Ⓚ
13. Ⓐ Ⓑ Ⓒ Ⓓ Ⓔ
14. Ⓕ Ⓖ Ⓗ Ⓙ Ⓚ
15. Ⓐ Ⓑ Ⓒ Ⓓ Ⓔ
16. Ⓕ Ⓖ Ⓗ Ⓙ Ⓚ

Teaching Resources

Name _____

Mark the space for the answer you have chosen.

1. Ⓐ Ⓑ Ⓒ Ⓓ Ⓔ	31. Ⓐ Ⓑ Ⓒ Ⓓ Ⓔ
2. Ⓕ Ⓖ Ⓗ Ⓙ Ⓚ	32. Ⓕ Ⓖ Ⓗ Ⓙ Ⓚ
3. Ⓐ Ⓑ Ⓒ Ⓓ Ⓔ	33. Ⓐ Ⓑ Ⓒ Ⓓ Ⓔ
4. Ⓕ Ⓖ Ⓗ Ⓙ Ⓚ	34. Ⓕ Ⓖ Ⓗ Ⓙ Ⓚ
5. Ⓐ Ⓑ Ⓒ Ⓓ Ⓔ	35. Ⓐ Ⓑ Ⓒ Ⓓ Ⓔ
6. Ⓕ Ⓖ Ⓗ Ⓙ Ⓚ	36. Ⓕ Ⓖ Ⓗ Ⓙ Ⓚ
7. Ⓐ Ⓑ Ⓒ Ⓓ Ⓔ	37. Ⓐ Ⓑ Ⓒ Ⓓ Ⓔ
8. Ⓕ Ⓖ Ⓗ Ⓙ Ⓚ	38. Ⓕ Ⓖ Ⓗ Ⓙ Ⓚ
9. Ⓐ Ⓑ Ⓒ Ⓓ Ⓔ	39. Ⓐ Ⓑ Ⓒ Ⓓ Ⓔ
10. Ⓕ Ⓖ Ⓗ Ⓙ Ⓚ	40. Ⓕ Ⓖ Ⓗ Ⓙ Ⓚ
11. Ⓐ Ⓑ Ⓒ Ⓓ Ⓔ	41. Ⓐ Ⓑ Ⓒ Ⓓ Ⓔ
12. Ⓕ Ⓖ Ⓗ Ⓙ Ⓚ	42. Ⓕ Ⓖ Ⓗ Ⓙ Ⓚ
13. Ⓐ Ⓑ Ⓒ Ⓓ Ⓔ	43. Ⓐ Ⓑ Ⓒ Ⓓ Ⓔ
14. Ⓕ Ⓖ Ⓗ Ⓙ Ⓚ	44. Ⓕ Ⓖ Ⓗ Ⓙ Ⓚ
15. Ⓐ Ⓑ Ⓒ Ⓓ Ⓔ	45. Ⓐ Ⓑ Ⓒ Ⓓ Ⓔ
16. Ⓕ Ⓖ Ⓗ Ⓙ Ⓚ	46. Ⓕ Ⓖ Ⓗ Ⓙ Ⓚ
17. Ⓐ Ⓑ Ⓒ Ⓓ Ⓔ	47. Ⓐ Ⓑ Ⓒ Ⓓ Ⓔ
18. Ⓕ Ⓖ Ⓗ Ⓙ Ⓚ	48. Ⓕ Ⓖ Ⓗ Ⓙ Ⓚ
19. Ⓐ Ⓑ Ⓒ Ⓓ Ⓔ	49. Ⓐ Ⓑ Ⓒ Ⓓ Ⓔ
20. Ⓕ Ⓖ Ⓗ Ⓙ Ⓚ	50. Ⓕ Ⓖ Ⓗ Ⓙ Ⓚ
21. Ⓐ Ⓑ Ⓒ Ⓓ Ⓔ	51. Ⓐ Ⓑ Ⓒ Ⓓ Ⓔ
22. Ⓕ Ⓖ Ⓗ Ⓙ Ⓚ	52. Ⓕ Ⓖ Ⓗ Ⓙ Ⓚ
23. Ⓐ Ⓑ Ⓒ Ⓓ Ⓔ	53. Ⓐ Ⓑ Ⓒ Ⓓ Ⓔ
24. Ⓕ Ⓖ Ⓗ Ⓙ Ⓚ	54. Ⓕ Ⓖ Ⓗ Ⓙ Ⓚ
25. Ⓐ Ⓑ Ⓒ Ⓓ Ⓔ	55. Ⓐ Ⓑ Ⓒ Ⓓ Ⓔ
26. Ⓕ Ⓖ Ⓗ Ⓙ Ⓚ	56. Ⓕ Ⓖ Ⓗ Ⓙ Ⓚ
27. Ⓐ Ⓑ Ⓒ Ⓓ Ⓔ	57. Ⓐ Ⓑ Ⓒ Ⓓ Ⓔ
28. Ⓕ Ⓖ Ⓗ Ⓙ Ⓚ	58. Ⓕ Ⓖ Ⓗ Ⓙ Ⓚ
29. Ⓐ Ⓑ Ⓒ Ⓓ Ⓔ	59. Ⓐ Ⓑ Ⓒ Ⓓ Ⓔ
30. Ⓕ Ⓖ Ⓗ Ⓙ Ⓚ	60. Ⓕ Ⓖ Ⓗ Ⓙ Ⓚ

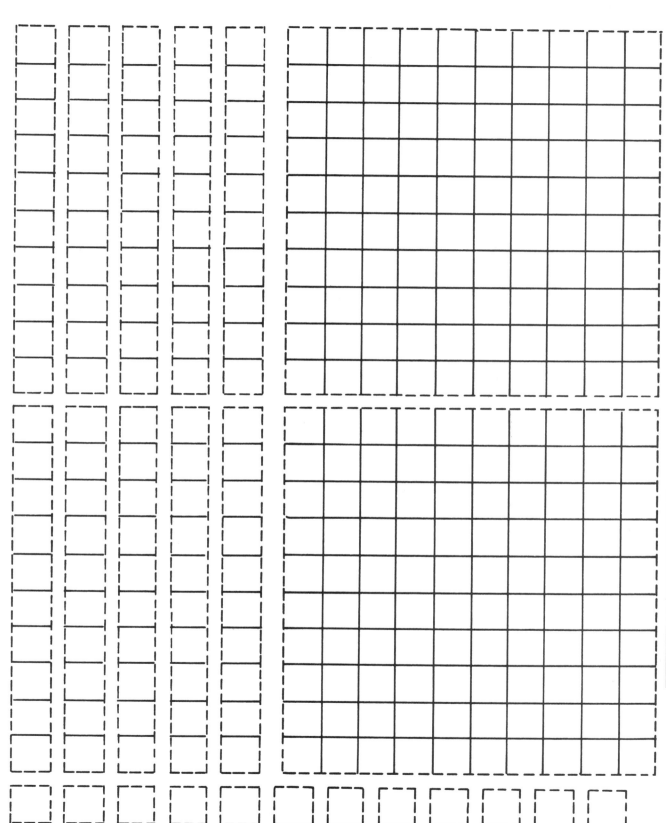

Teaching Resources

Millions			Thousands			Ones		
hundreds	tens	ones	hundreds	tens	ones	hundreds	tens	ones

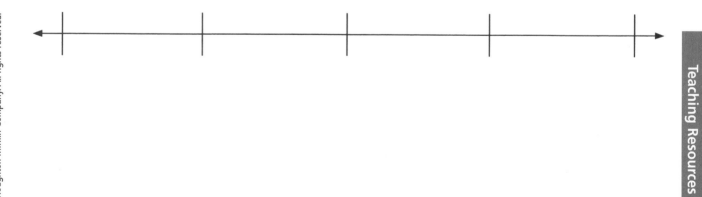

Teaching Resources

1	2	3	4	5	6	7	8	9	10
11	12	13	14	15	16	17	18	19	20
21	22	23	24	25	26	27	28	29	30
31	32	33	34	35	36	37	38	39	40
41	42	43	44	45	46	47	48	49	50
51	52	53	54	55	56	57	58	59	60
61	62	63	64	65	66	67	68	69	70
71	72	73	74	75	76	77	78	79	80
81	82	83	84	85	86	87	88	89	90
91	92	93	94	95	96	97	98	99	100

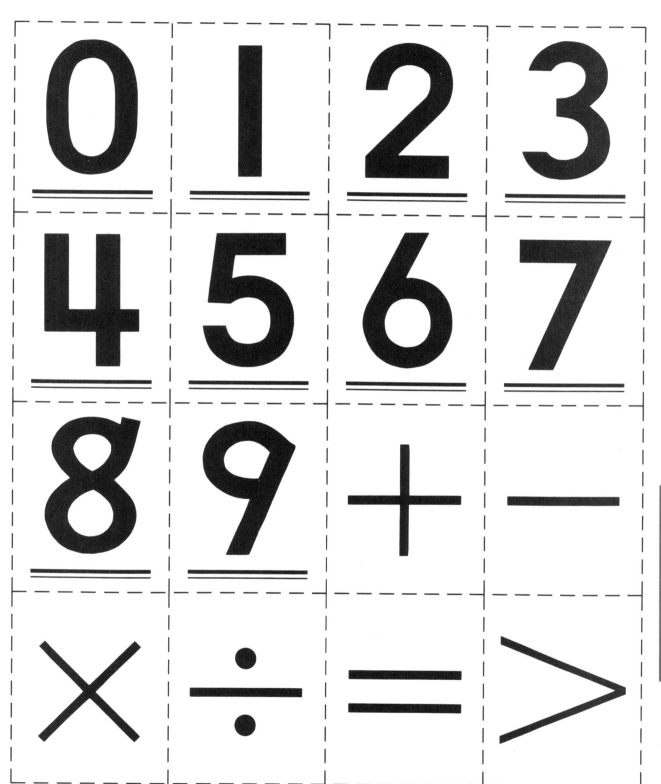

Teaching Resources

×	0	1	2	3	4	5	6	7	8	9	10
0											
1											
2											
3											
4											
5											
6											
7											
8											
9											
10											

5 ×2	2 ×3	4 ×0	3 ×3	2 ×4	4 ×8
3 ×4	5 ×6	4 ×4	3 ×2	5 ×5	4 ×3
4 ×2	1 ×6	2 ×5	5 ×4	2 ×6	3 ×5
4 ×5	2 ×7	5 ×9	3 ×6	5 ×8	4 ×9
3 ×7	4 ×6	5 ×3	2 ×8	3 ×8	0 ×7
2 ×9	5 ×7	4 ×1	1 ×9	4 ×7	3 ×9

Teaching Resources

8 ×2	6 ×3	8 ×8	7 ×0	8 ×5	7 ×2
6 ×4	7 ×6	9 ×2	6 ×8	9 ×9	9 ×5
9 ×3	6 ×9	7 ×3	8 ×4	6 ×1	9 ×8
7 ×5	8 ×6	6 ×2	7 ×7	9 ×7	8 ×9
8 ×1	6 ×6	9 ×4	7 ×8	9 ×6	6 ×5
8 ×7	7 ×9	6 ×7	8 ×3	9 ×0	7 ×4

$5\overline{)40}$	$3\overline{)15}$	$2\overline{)10}$	$4\overline{)24}$	$2\overline{)2}$	$5\overline{)25}$
$3\overline{)24}$	$2\overline{)18}$	$4\overline{)4}$	$5\overline{)5}$	$3\overline{)12}$	$4\overline{)28}$
$5\overline{)45}$	$4\overline{)36}$	$5\overline{)30}$	$2\overline{)12}$	$4\overline{)8}$	$2\overline{)8}$
$3\overline{)3}$	$4\overline{)12}$	$3\overline{)21}$	$4\overline{)32}$	$5\overline{)10}$	$3\overline{)18}$
$5\overline{)20}$	$2\overline{)4}$	$5\overline{)35}$	$2\overline{)14}$	$3\overline{)9}$	$4\overline{)16}$
$3\overline{)6}$	$4\overline{)20}$	$2\overline{)16}$	$5\overline{)15}$	$2\overline{)6}$	$3\overline{)27}$

Teaching Resources

6)24	9)81	8)56	9)36	8)64	7)35
7)63	8)32	6)48	7)7	6)18	8)40
9)9	7)28	8)8	9)63	7)42	9)18
6)30	9)54	7)14	6)42	9)72	7)56
7)21	6)6	9)45	8)72	8)24	6)36
8)16	9)27	6)12	7)49	6)54	8)48

Name _____

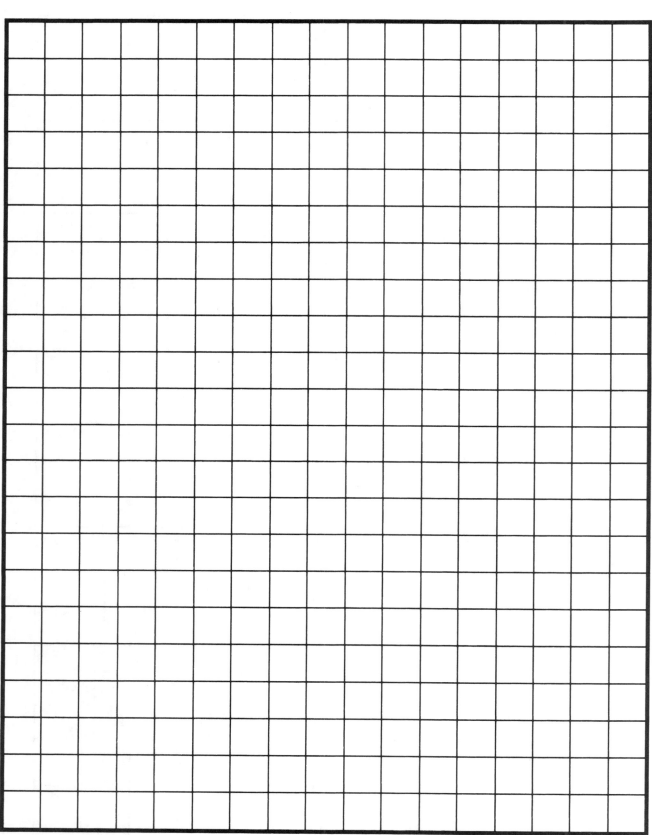

Teaching Resources

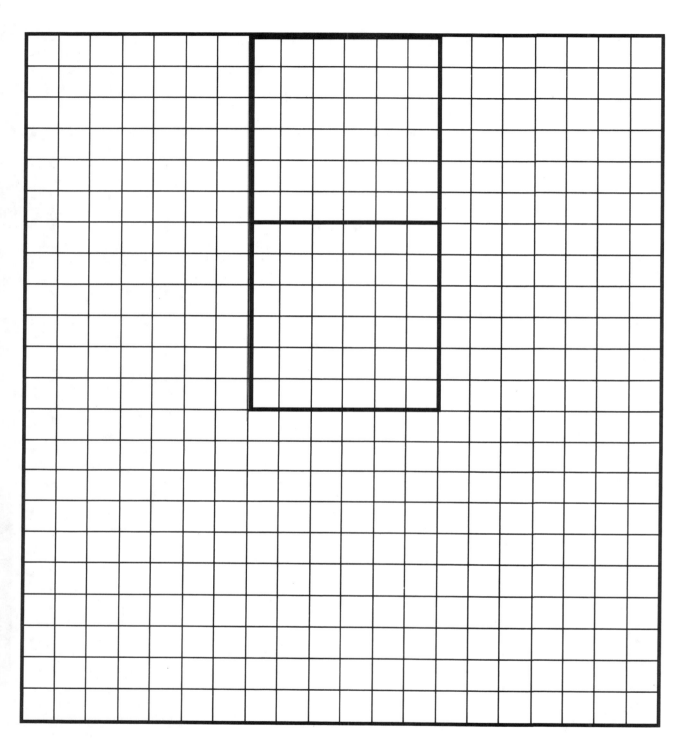

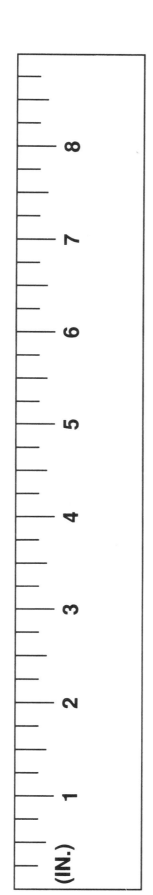

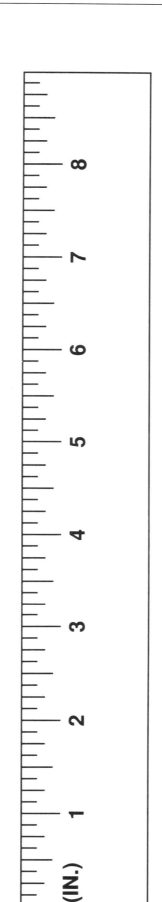

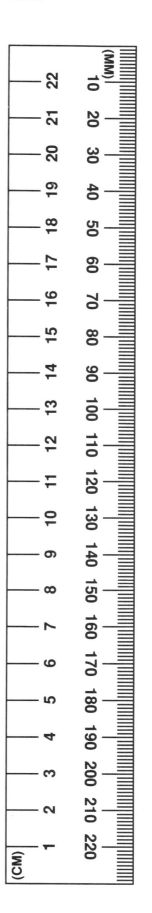

Teaching Resources

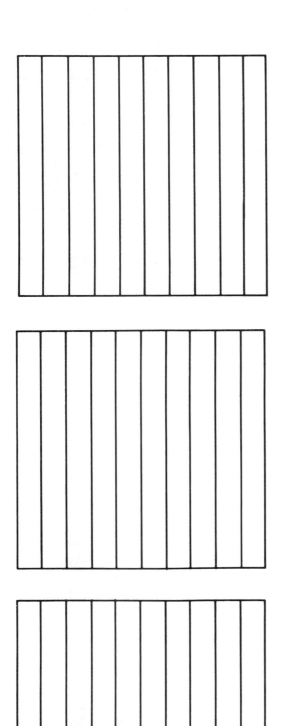

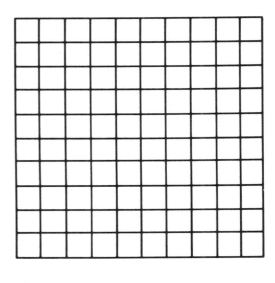

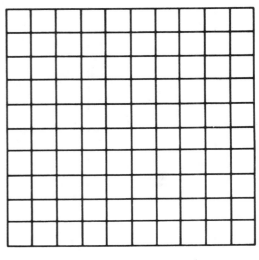

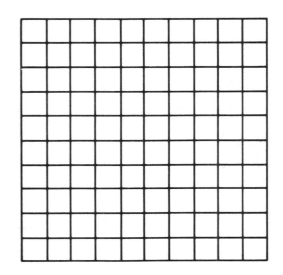

hundreds	tens	ones	tenths	hundredths
		.		
		.		
		.		

hundreds	tens	ones	tenths	hundredths
		.		
		.		
		.		

hundreds	tens	ones	tenths	hundredths
		.		
		.		
		.		

hundreds	tens	ones	tenths	hundredths
		.		
		.		
		.		

hundreds	tens	ones	tenths	hundredths
		.		
		.		
		.		

hundreds	tens	ones	tenths	hundredths
		.		
		.		
		.		

Teaching Resources

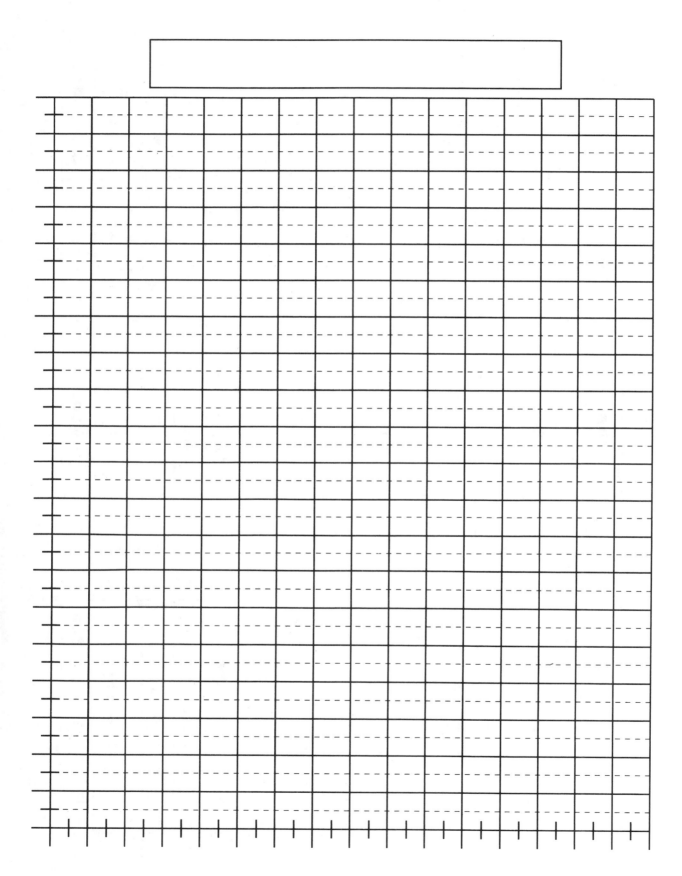

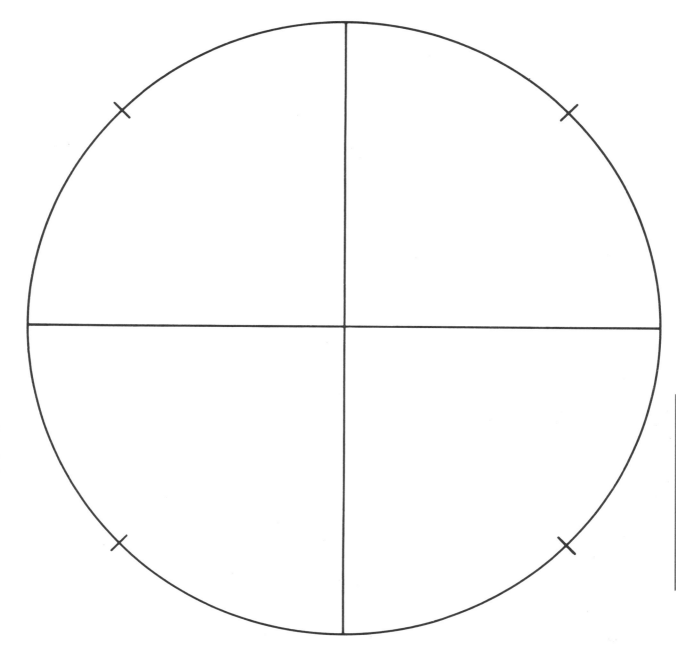

Teaching Resources

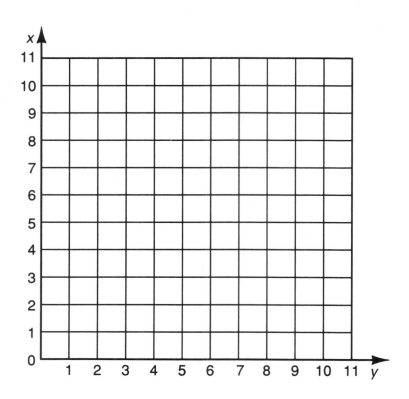

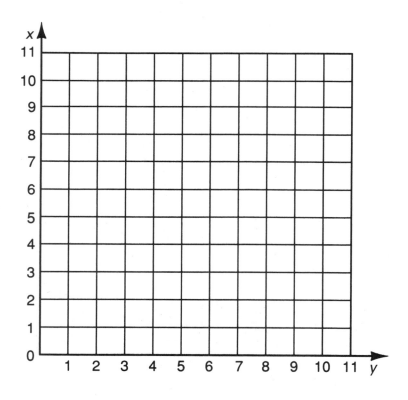

Cut out the cards on this page to do the activity.

1 This Mystery Number has 2 ones, 4 hundreds, 6 ten thousands, 8 millions. The only other digit is 0.	**2** This Mystery Number has 4 tens, 2 hundreds, 8 ten thousands, 6 millions. The only other digit is 0.	**3** This Mystery Number has 2 thousands, 6 ten thousands, 8 hundred thousands, 4 millions. The only other digit is 0.
4 This Mystery Number has 4 tens, 2 one thousands, 6 hundred thousands. The only other digit is 1. It is less than one million.	**5** This Mystery Number has 6 tens, 4 thousands, 2 ten thousands, 8 hundred thousands. The only other digit is 1. It is less than one million.	**6** This Mystery Number has 8 tens, 2 hundreds, 6 ten thousands, 4 hundred thousands. The only other digit is 1. It is less than one million.
7 This Mystery Number has 6 hundreds, 4 thousands, 2 ten thousands, 8 millions. The only other digit is 0.	**8** This Mystery Number has 8 ones, 6 thousands, 4 ten thousands, 2 hundred thousands. The only other digit is 0.	**9** This Mystery Number has 4 tens, 8 thousands, 6 ten thousands, 2 millions. The only other digit is 0.
a 6,080,240	b 461,281	c 612,141
d 2,068,040	e 8,060,402	f 4, 862,000
g 246,008	h 8,024,600	i 824,161

✂ -

Family Note:
- Cut out the cards above to help your student with place value.
- Play a game in which the goal is to get pairs of cards where one card is the mystery number description and the other card is the mystery number.
  Put the small and large cards in separate groups face down. Each player takes a turn, turning over a small and a big card. When a match is made, the player keeps both cards.
- When all the cards are used, the player with the most cards wins.

Answers: 1-e, 2-a, 3-f, 4-c, 5-I, 6-b, 7-h, 8-g, 9-d

Family Projects

Cut out the cards on this page to do the activity.

Bell School District
Revere School: **1,363** students
Washington School: **2,564** students

Carlton School District
Jefferson School: **985** students
Adams School: **1,582** students

_____

_____

_____

_____

Movie Attendance: Stanford Theater
Friday: **1,932** people
Saturday: **2,587** people

Movie Attendance: Central Theater
Friday: **967** people
Saturday: **1,549** people

_____

_____

_____

_____

Smith Family Trip
Day 1: 352 miles
Day 2: 476 miles
Day 3: 132 miles

Hart Family Trip
Day 1: 296 miles
Day 2: 135 miles
Day 3: 276 miles

_____

_____

_____

_____

Daily News
Week 1: 1,673 newspapers sold
Week 2: 2,154 newspapers sold

Alltown Times
Week 1: 5,756 newspapers sold
Week 2: 6,134 newspapers sold

_____

_____

_____

_____

✂ -

Family Note:
- Cut out the cards above.
- Each day have your child choose one of the cards. Ask him or her to write a problem that involves both addition and subtraction.
- Ask your child to solve the problem.
- Review the problem with your child—check that the mathematics, grammar, punctuation, and spelling are correct. Have your child correct any errors he or she has made.
- An example of a problem follows:
  Attendance at the Central Zoo on Monday was 1,732 people. On Tuesday, the attendance was 2,346 people. On Monday, attendance at the Aquarium was 3,562 people. On Tuesday it was 2,651 people. Which attraction had more visitors altogether for the two days? How many more?
  Answer: The Aquarium had more visitors; 2,135 more visitors

Cut out the cards on this page to do the activity.

A 495 × 10	B 495 × 100	C 28 × 10
D 28 × 100	E 70 × 80	F 80 × 40
G 20 × 80	H 20 × 50	I 100 × 100
R 5,600	S 49,500	T 1,600
U 2,800	V 1,500	W 4,950
X 3,200	Y 280	Z 10,000

✂ -

Family Note:
- Cut out the cards above to help your child with multiplication of whole numbers.
- Play a game in which the goal is to get pairs of cards where one card is the multiplication problem and the other card is the answer.
- Place the cards face down in 6 rows of 3 cards. Each player takes a turn turning over 2 cards. When a match is made, the player keeps both cards.
- When all the cards are used, the player with the most cards wins.

Answers: A-W; B-S; C-Y; D-U; E-R; F-X; G-T; H-V; I-Z

Family Projects

Name _____

Cut out the cards on this page to do the activity.

7×5	8×6	6×2	7×7	9×7	8×9
8×1	6×6	9×4	7×8	9×6	6×5
8×7	7×9	6×7	8×3	9×0	7×4
$4\overline{)24}$	$4\overline{)24}$	$2\overline{)12}$	$4\overline{)32}$	$2\overline{)14}$	$5\overline{)15}$
$2\overline{)2}$	$3\overline{)12}$	$4\overline{)8}$	$5\overline{)10}$	$3\overline{)9}$	$2\overline{)6}$
$5\overline{)25}$	$4\overline{)28}$	$2\overline{)8}$	$3\overline{)18}$	$4\overline{)16}$	$3\overline{)27}$

Family Note:
Cut out the cards above to help your child with multiplication and division basic facts. Ask him or her to write the answer on the back of each card. Use the cards as flash cards to practice multiplication and division basic facts.

Find the error. Then solve the problem.

① $\frac{3}{5} + \frac{1}{5} = \frac{4}{10}$	**②** $\frac{4}{7} - \frac{1}{7} = \frac{3}{0}$
③ $\frac{3}{8} - 2\frac{1}{8} = 3\frac{2}{0}$	**④** $5\frac{1}{3} + 2\frac{1}{3} = 7\frac{2}{6}$
⑤ $\frac{3}{8} - \frac{1}{4} = \frac{2}{4}$	**⑥** $\frac{1}{2} + \frac{1}{3} = \frac{2}{5}$

✂ -

Family Note:
Do this activity to help your child understand addition and subtraction of fractions. Every problem on this page has been solved incorrectly. Ask your child to find the error that was made and then solve the problem.

Answers:
1. Error: Adding the denominators instead of writing the common denominator; $\frac{4}{5}$ **2.** Error: Subtracting the denominators instead of writing the common denominator; $\frac{3}{7}$ **3.** Error: Subtracting the denominators instead of writing the common denominator; $3\frac{1}{4}$ **4.** Error: Adding the denominators instead of writing the common denominator; $7\frac{2}{3}$ **5.** Error: Not finding common denominator before subtracting; $\frac{1}{8}$ **6.** Error: Not finding common denominator before adding; $\frac{5}{6}$

Family Projects

Cut out the figures. Find the number of lines of symmetry for each figure.

1

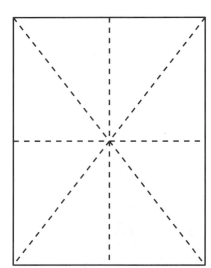

2

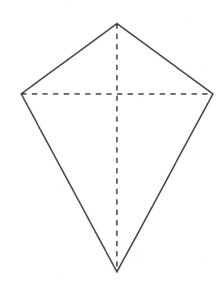

3

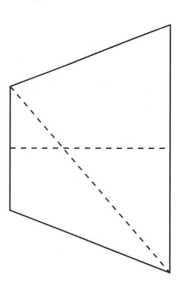

4

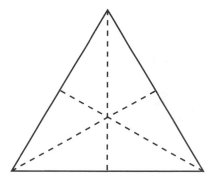

✂ -

Family Note:
Ask your child to cut out the figures above. Then have your child fold the figure along one of the dotted lines to see if it is a line of symmetry. If it is, then the 2 parts of the figure should match and your child should trace along the line with a pencil. Be sure your child unfolds the figure before folding along the next dotted line.

Answers:
1. 2 lines of symmetry   2. 1 line of symmetry   3. 1 line of symmetry 4. 3 lines of symmetry

Cut out the cards on this page to do the activity.
Measure to the nearest quarter inch.

Length of a pencil _____inches	Width of a door _____feet	Width of a bed _____inches
Length of a toothbrush _____inches	Length of a table _____feet	Length of a piece of paper _____inches
Length of a fork _____inches	Length of your shoe _____inches	Length of a family member's shoe _____inches
Height of a glass _____inches	Length of an envelope _____inches	Height of a door _____feet

✂ ▬

Family Note:
• Cut out the cards above to help your student with measurement.
• Each day, ask your child to choose 2 cards.
• Have your child use an inch ruler or a yardstick to measure and record the length of the object on the card.
• Check that your child is aligning the correct end of the ruler with an end of the object.
• Then verify that your child is reading the correct mark on the ruler to the nearest $\frac{1}{4}$ inch.

Family Projects

Ask a family member these questions about how they use decimals.

1. How do you use decimals when you go to the grocery store?

_____

_____

_____

2. How do you use decimals when you go to the bank?

_____

_____

_____

3. How do you use decimals at work?

_____

_____

_____

4. How do you use decimals when you go on a trip or vacation?

_____

_____

_____

5. What are other ways that you use decimals?

_____

_____

_____

✂ -

Family Note:
Use this questionnaire to help your child understand how decimals are used in everyday life. Have your child ask these questions to at least one adult family member and fill out the survey as the questions are answered.
Examples: **1.** prices of items **2.** deposits or withdrawals **3.** amount of pay received **4.** cost of gasoline
5. cost of clothing, electricity, fuel oil

Find the error. Then solve the problem.

①

$$20R25$$
$$28\overline{)81}$$
$$\underline{-56}$$
$$25$$

②

$$20R7$$
$$42\overline{)913}$$
$$\underline{-84}$$
$$7$$

③

$$2$$
$$36\overline{)720}$$
$$\underline{-72}$$
$$0$$

④

$$94$$
$$23\overline{)2164}$$
$$\underline{-207}$$
$$94$$
$$\underline{-92}$$
$$2$$

✂ -- -- -- -- -- -- -- -- -- -- -- -- -- -- -- -- -- ✂ -- --

Family Note:
Do this activity to help your child understand division with 2-digit divisors. Every problem on this page has been solved incorrectly. Ask your child to find the error that was made and then solve the problem.

Answers: 1. Error: Put the first 2 in the wrong place in the quotient. Should be above the 1 in 81; 2R25
2. Error: Did not bring down the 3 and then divide by 42 again; 21R31 **3.** Error: Did not bring down the 0 and then record a zero in the quoient; 20 **4.** Error: Forgot to write remainder; 94 R2

Family Projects

Name _____

**Complete the table that shows the results of a class survey.
Then answer the questions.**

Number of Letters in First Names

Number of Letters	Tally	Total Number of Students
Three	Ⲏ	
Four	Ⲏ Ⲏ ‖	
Five	Ⲏ ‖	
Six	‖‖	

Some of Our Names
Ann   Billy
Carol
Miguel   Joel
Kate
John   Leah

1.a. How many students were surveyed altogether? _____

  b. How did you find the total? _____

2.a. Which number of letters had the most votes? _____

  How many votes did it have? _____

  b. Which number of letters had the fewest votes?_____

  How many votes did it have? _____

  c. Use < or > to compare the fewest to the greatest number of votes.

  _____

3. Use the data from the tally chart. Complete
the line plot. Then answer the questions.

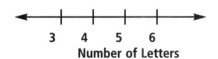

3   4   5   6
Number of Letters

  a. What is the median?_____

  Is there a mode?_____ If so, what is it? _____

  b. Is there an outlier?_____ If so what is it?_____

✂ -

Family Note:

Use the survey above to help your child understand surveys and line plots. Extend the activity by having your child take a survey of his or her choice and answer similar questions about it.

Answers: Total number of people who voted: Three Letters 5; Four Letters 12, Five Letters 7; Six Letters 3
1. a. 27 students were surveyed. **b.** Found the sum of the number who voted for each number of letters
2. a. Four Letters, 12; **b.** Six Letters, 3; **c.** 12 > 3 or 3 < 12
3. a. Since there are an odd number of data items, the median is the middle number when the data are arranged from least to greatest. The median is 4. The mode is the number that occurs most often—the mode is 4.
3. b. An outlier is a number that is much greater or less than the other numbers in the data set. This data set does not have an outlier.

Name _____

Describe the rule using words. Then complete the table.

1. _____   2. _____

_____   _____

cars (c)	wheels (w)
1	4
2	8
3	12
4	

chickens (c)	legs (l)
1	2
2	4
3	6
4	

3. _____   4. _____

_____   _____

weeks (w)	days (d)
1	7
2	14
3	21
4	
5	

cups (c)	plates (p)
3	5
6	8
9	11
12	
15	

✂ -

Family Note:
Have your child find the rule and complete the function tables. A function is a rule that uses operations and "input" numbers to find the "output" numbers. In the tables above, the first column represents the input numbers and the second, the output.

Answers: 1. The number of wheels is four times the number of cars; 16
2. The number of legs is two times the number of chickens; 8
3. The number of days is seven times the number of weeks: 28, 35
4. The number of plates is 2 more than the number of cups; 14,17

Family Projects

Answer Keys

NOTES

Answer Key
Beginning of the Year Inventory

1. square
2. pentagon
3. trapezoid
4. octagon
5. hexagon
6. parallelogram
7. triangle
8. rectangle
9. ones
10. tens
11. hundreds
12. thousands
13. ten-thousands
14. forty thousand, five hundred ninety-eight
15. 826,325
16. 93,709
17. 6,300,411
18. 64,325
19. 3,580,902
20. 1,074,000
21. 4
22. 5
23. 1
24. 0
25. 1
26. 6
27. B, C
28. D, E
29. B, C, D, E
30. unlikely
31. likely
32. impossible
33. certain
34. $\frac{3}{5}$
35. $\frac{2}{2}$
36. $\frac{5}{6}$
37. $\frac{1}{4}$
38. $\frac{4}{10}$
39. $\frac{5}{5}$
40. 2
41. 9
42. 4
43. D
44. A
45. $2\frac{1}{3}$
46. $1\frac{7}{8}$
47. 0.3

48. 0.75
49. 12
50. 1
51. 3
52. <
53. >
54. >
55. 60
56. 720
57. 5,770
58. 20
59. 400
60. 7,000
61. 28
62. 40
63. 25
64. 88
65. $69
66. 527
67. 2.1
68. $4.89
69. $8.98
70. 520
71. 6,429
72. 8,094
73. 57
74. 237
75. $2.51
76. 5,334
77. 21
78. 45
79. 4
80. 8
81. 6
82. 6
83. 8
84. 64
85. 8
86. 0
87. 70
88. 680
89. <
90. >
91. >
92. $\frac{1}{8}, \frac{1}{4}, \frac{1}{2}, \frac{1}{1}$
93. $\frac{2}{5}, \frac{2}{3}, \frac{2}{2}, \frac{2}{1}$
94. $\frac{2}{3}$
95. $\frac{3}{5}$
96. $\frac{2}{4}$

Answer Key
Beginning of the Year Inventory

97. $\frac{4}{8}$
98. 0.3
99. 0.29
100. 0.5
101. 7 R3, 7 × 4 + 3 = 31
102. 6 R2, 6 × 6 + 2 = 38
103. 32, 32 × 3 = 96
104. 106, 106 × 8 = 848
105. $2.05, $2.05 × 6 = $12.30
106. $2.49, $2.49 × 2 = $4.98
107. 88
108. 1,245
109. $6.70
110. 4,682
111. $9.75
112. $20.25
113. area: 12, perimeter: 14
114. area: 8, perimeter: 14
115. $.28
116. 5
117. $19
118. 362
119. 1 = 4 + 10, 1 = 14 inches
120. t = 2 × 32, t = 64 inches
121. 3
122. Yantz
123. 4

Answer Key • Pretests and Posttests

Unit 1 Pretest
1. 5,724
2. 84,907
3. 762,011
4. 4,300,001
5. 590,071,610
6. <
7. >
8. <
9. <
10. >
11. =
12. 300
13. 31,200
14. 60,000
15. 860,000
16. 2,700,000
17. 8,400,000
18. minus 1, plus 1
19. 3 hours

Unit 1 Posttest
1. 7,978
2. 45,208
3. 324,050
4. 8,100,006
5. 920,032,412
6. >
7. <
8. >
9. <
10. =
11. <
12. 600
13. 56,900
14. 50,000
15. 350,000
16. 0
17. 6,600,000
18. minus 3, plus 3
19. 2 days

Unit 2 Pretest
1. 3
2. 7
3. 9
4. 14
5. 0
6. 8
7. 9 + 6 = 15
8. 4 + 11 = 15
9. 10, 10 − 4 = 6
10. 8, 8 + 5 = 13
11. 8, 8 + 8 = 16
12. 50 + 20 = 70

(Unit 2 Pretest continued)
13. 600 − 300 = 300
14. 600 + 300 = 900
15. 618
16. $53.60
17. 30,691
18. 72,682
19. $5, $2.55, $2.45
20. $1.75 + $6.50 = $8.25
21. $5.02

Unit 2 Posttest
1. 6
2. 3
3. 8
4. 0
5. 1
6. 17
7. 9 + 6 = 15
8. 1 + 14 = 15
9. 7, 7 − 5 = 2
10. 9, 9 + 9 = 18
11. 4, 4 + 8 = 12
12. 80 + 30 = 110
13. 800 − 400 = 400
14. 9,000 + 4,000 = 13,000
15. 918
16. $48.63
17. 53,079
18. 28,168
19. $5, $3.60, $1.40
20. $7.95 + $1.25 = $9.20
21. $9.02

Unit 3 Pretest
1. 16
2. 0
3. 3
4. 252
5. 186
6. 3,704
7. 24,856
8. 150
9. $28.08
10. $82.25
11. 54,000
12. 350
13. 8,074
14. 80 × 4 = 320
15. 50 × 20 = 1,000
16. $8 × 50 = $400
17. $1.50 and $3
18. Lukas
19. 26

Unit 3 Posttest
1. 40
2. 0
3. 5
4. 125
5. 188
6. 1,432
7. 32,550
8. 1,200
9. $16.52
10. $96.46
11. 4,000
12. 1,824
13. 5,980
14. 50 × 8 = 400
15. 80 × 20 = 1,600
16. $5 × 70 = $350
17. $4.20, $2.10
18. 6
19. 69

Unit 4 Pretest
1. 21
2. 30
3. 6
4. 5 R5
5. 84 R1
6. $1.49
7. 881 R2
8. 12, 24, 60
9. 30, 45, 90
10. 1×16, $\underline{2} \times 8$, 4×4
11. 1×32, $\underline{2} \times 16$, 4×8
12. $1 \times \underline{37}$
13. 1×54, $\underline{2} \times 27$, $\underline{3} \times 18$, 6×9
14. 5
15. 35
16. $.30
17. $10
18. $.55

Unit 4 Posttest
1. 45
2. 10
3. 10
4. 5 R7
5. 79 R6
6. $1.22
7. 844 R1
8. 30, 60, 80
9. 24, 36, 66
10. 1×18, 2×9, $\underline{3} \times 6$
11. 1×63, $\underline{3} \times 21$, 7×9
12. 1×40, $\underline{2} \times 20$, 4×10, 5×8
13. $1 \times \underline{53}$

(Unit 4 Posttest continued)
14. 7
15. 27
16. $.31
17. $10
18. $1.75

Unit 5 Pretest
1. <u>12</u>, 16, 20, <u>24</u>, 28, 32, <u>36</u>, 40, 44

   <u>12</u>, 18, <u>24</u>, 30, <u>36</u>, 42, 48, 54, 60
2. $\frac{4}{5}$
3. $\frac{1}{3}$
4. <
5. =
6. $\frac{1}{3}$, $\frac{1}{2}$, $\frac{3}{4}$, $\frac{5}{6}$
7. $\frac{3}{1}$
8. $\frac{11}{3}$
9. $\frac{1}{4}$
10. $\frac{5}{7}$
11. $3\frac{3}{5}$
12. $1\frac{1}{4}$
13. $\frac{5}{8}$
14. $\frac{9}{10}$
15. $\frac{1}{2}$
16. $\frac{3}{8}$
17. $1\frac{1}{4}$ apples
18. Possible answer:

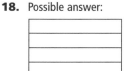

Unit 5 Posttest
1. 10, 15, <u>20</u>, 25, 30, 35, <u>40</u>, 45, 50

   12, 16, <u>20</u>, 24, 28, 32, 36, <u>40</u>, 44
2. $\frac{2}{3}$
3. $\frac{3}{5}$
4. <
5. >
6. $\frac{1}{4}$, $\frac{1}{2}$, $\frac{5}{8}$, $\frac{2}{3}$

Answer Keys

Answer Key • Pretests and Posttests

(Unit 5 Posttest continued)

7. $\frac{5}{1}$

8. $\frac{14}{5}$

9. $\frac{2}{7}$

10. $1\frac{1}{3}$

11. $2\frac{4}{5}$

12. $2\frac{1}{2}$

13. $\frac{3}{4}$

14. $1\frac{1}{6}$

15. $\frac{1}{8}$

16. $\frac{1}{6}$

17. $1\frac{2}{3}$

18. Possible answer:

Unit 6 Pretest

1. *AB*
2. *RS ∥ TU*
3. ray *MN*
4. ∠ *CDE* or ∠ *EDC*
5. *A* and *C*
6. *B* and *F*
7. obtuse
8. acute
9. right
10. *LO, NO,* or *MO*
11. *LM*
12. quarter, 90°
13. three quarter, 270°
14. half, 180°
15. full, 360°
16. trapezoid
17. parallelogram
18. rectangular prism
19. cylinder
20. No.
21. Yes.
22. No.
23. Yes.
24. Possible answer:

(Unit 6 Pretest continued)

25. brand A
26. rectangle, parallelogram, kite-shaped figure

Unit 6 Posttest

1. *FG*
2. *KL ∥ MN*
3. ray *ST*
4. ∠ *XYZ* or ∠ *ZYX*
5. *A* and *D*
6. *B* and *E*
7. acute
8. obtuse
9. right
10. *OQ, OR,* or *OS*
11. *QS*
12. half, 180°
13. full, 360°
14. quarter, 90°
15. three quarter, 270°
16. rhombus
17. trapezoid
18. triangular prism
19. cube
20. Yes.
21. No.
22. No.
23. Yes.
24.

25. red
26. an acute triangle and an obtuse triangle

Unit 7 Pretest

1. 5 in., $5\frac{1}{2}$ in.
2. 7 cm, 73 mm
3. 2 gal
4. 1 L
5. 1 lb
6. 1 kg
7. 8
8. 48 oz
9. 15 ft
10. 2
11. 6,000
12. 1
13. 70
14. 8,000
15. 2 L
16. 3

(Unit 7 Pretest continued)

17. 5,000
18. 4
19. D
20. C
21. R
22. T
23. 18
24. 14
25. 16
26. 15
27. 16
28. 13
29. 54
30. 27
31. 94
32. 60
33. S and A
34. 9:45 P.M.

Unit 7 Posttest

1. 4 in., $3\frac{1}{2}$ in.
2. 11 cm, 108 mm
3. 2 qt
4. 5 L
5. 1 oz
6. 1 kg
7. 18
8. 9,000
9. 2
10. 1
11. 12,000
12. 10,560
13. 20
14. 80
15. 5
16. 90
17. 4,000
18. 3
19. R
20. P
21. B
22. W
23. 20
24. 21
25. 20
26. 16
27. 16
28. 12
29. 40
30. 16
31. 110
32. 75
33. A and J
34. 10:00 P.M.

Unit 8 Pretest 8

1. three and nine hundredths
2. six tenths
3. 0.4
4. 3.3
5. 0.25
6. 5.5
7. $\frac{7}{10}$
8. $9\frac{7}{100}$
9. $5\frac{9}{10}$
10. <
11. =
12. >
13. 2.55, 2.15, 1.4, 0.7, 0.2
14. 5.2
15. 1.8
16. 12.9
17. 18.5
18. 8
19. 2
20. 16
21. 15
22. 19.63
23. 3.41
24. 14.49
25. 6.04
26. 0.25
27. a group of 15 hikers; 12 hikers

Unit 8 Posttest

1. seven and five hundredths
2. nine tenths
3. 0.9
4. 7.6
5. 0.25
6. 4.75
7. $\frac{9}{10}$
8. $14\frac{7}{100}$
9. $2\frac{1}{10}$
10. <
11. <
12. =
13. 2.15, 2.1, 1.25, 0.5, 0.3
14. 7.4
15. 4.4
16. 11.8
17. 12.2
18. 3
19. 8
20. 13
21. 18
22. 19.72

Answer Key • Pretests and Posttests

(Unit 8 Posttest continued)
23. 2.42
24. 10.24
25. 2.18
26. 2
27. a group of 28 campers; 25 campers

Unit 9 Pretest
1. 6
2. 1 R13
3. 7 R21
4. 30
5. 91 R9
6. 212 R24
7. 208
8. 410 R5
9. 125 R38
10. 60, 360, 6
11. 25; 7,500; 300
12. 72 balloons, 18 stuffed animals
13. 15 pieces

Unit 9 Posttest
1. 6
2. 1 R19
3. 5 R12
4. 40
5. 49 R4
6. 207 R29
7. 306
8. 451 R10
9. 166 R4
10. 70, 280, 4
11. 25; 5,000; 200
12. waters 20 times; mows the lawn 12 times
13. 10

Unit 10 Pretest
1. range: $92 - 27 = 65$, median: 41, mode: 41, outlier: 92
2. range: $75 - 12 = 63$, median: 69, mode: 68, outlier: 12
3.–5.

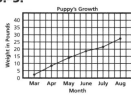

(Unit 10 Pretest continued)
6. July
7. The puppy gained 5 pounds.
8. 3 out of 6
9. spinner pointing to a square
10.

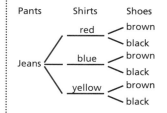

11. 6
12. $4\frac{1}{2}$ pt strawberries; $2\frac{1}{4}$ c blackberries; 3 pt blueberries; 1 qt cranberry juice; 2 qt vanilla yogurt
13. strawberries, $4\frac{1}{2}$ pt

Unit 10 Posttest
1. range: $84 - 26 = 58$, median: 33, mode: 26, outlier: 84
2. range: $64 - 5 = 59$, median: 54, no mode, outlier: 5
3.–5.

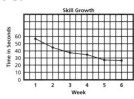

6. week 1 and week 2
7. It decreased by 4 seconds.
8. 1 out of 8
9. the spinner pointing to a star
10.

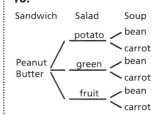

(Unit 10 Posttest continued)
11. 6
12. $6\frac{1}{2}$ qt tangerine juice; 7 pt strawberries; $1\frac{1}{2}$ pt mango juice; $3\frac{1}{4}$ c pineapple; 2 pt blackberries
13. tangerine juice, $6\frac{1}{2}$ qt

Unit 11 Pretest
For Exercises 1–3, accept any appropriate variables.
1. $n, n - 3$
2. $n, \frac{n}{4}$
3. $n, 3n$
4. 6
5. 30
6. 8
7. 15
8. 7
9. 35
10. 7
11. 37
12. $n + 3 = 12, n = 9$
13. $n + 14 = 30, n = 16$
14. $\frac{n}{8} = 3, n = 24$
15. $n - x = 13, n = x + 13$
16. $n - 6 = 12, n = 18$
17. $2 \times n = 24, n = 12$
18.–20.

x	$x - 2$	y	
6	$6 - 2$	4	(6,4)
5	$5 - 2$	3	(5,3)
4	$4 - 2$	2	(4,2)
3	$3 - 2$	1	(3,1)

21. diagonal line segment

22. $w + 6 = 14, w = 8$
23. She gave the clerk $20. $18.35

Unit 11 Posttest
For Exercises 1–3, accept any appropriate variables.
1. $n, n - 8$
2. $r, 5r$
3. $w, 3w$
4. 8
5. 20
6. 8
7. 9
8. 7
9. 39
10. 9
11. 5
12. $n - 7 = 5, n = 12$
13. $h + 12 = 75, h = 63$
14. $n \times 7 = 56, n = 8$
15. $n \div 9 = 7, n = 63$
16. $n - 6 = 20, n = 26$
17. $3 \times n = 75, n = 25$
18.–20.

x	$x + 2$	y	
0	$0 + 2$	2	(0,2)
1	$1 + 2$	3	(1,3)
3	$3 + 2$	5	(3,5)
4	$4 + 2$	6	(4,6)

21. a line

22. 12 inches
23. Tickets to a concert cost $35. 2,220

Answer Key • Midyear Test

1.	B	26.	K
2.	G	27.	E
3.	D	28.	H
4.	F	29.	B
5.	B	30.	K
6.	F	31.	B
7.	B	32.	J
8.	H	33.	E
9.	A	34.	J
10.	F	35.	C
11.	D	36.	G
12.	G	37.	C
13.	D	38.	J
14.	J	39.	B
15.	C	40.	K
16.	G	41.	A
17.	B	42.	J
18.	H	43.	A
19.	B	44.	K
20.	G	45.	B
21.	C	46.	J
22.	F	47.	A
23.	B	48.	G
24.	J	49.	C
25.	D	50.	H

Answer Key • Final Test

1.	B		**27.**	B
2.	G		**28.**	J
3.	C		**29.**	B
4.	H		**30.**	H
5.	A		**31.**	C
6.	F		**32.**	K
7.	D		**33.**	C
8.	J		**34.**	H
9.	C		**35.**	B
10.	J		**36.**	H
11.	B		**37.**	E
12.	H		**38.**	F
13.	D		**39.**	D
14.	J		**40.**	H
15.	D		**41.**	A
16.	H		**42.**	H
17.	D		**43.**	C
18.	G		**44.**	H
19.	A		**45.**	C
20.	F		**46.**	H
21.	C		**47.**	C
22.	G		**48.**	K
23.	C		**49.**	A
24.	J		**50.**	H
25.	C		**51.**	A
26.	G		**52.**	J

Answer Keys

Answer Key • Reteach Worksheets

Reteach 1, page 59
1. 2,076; 2,000 + 70 + 6; two thousand seventy-six
2. 30
3. 300
4. 3,000
5. 300
6. 3
7. 52; 50 + 2
8. 8,700; 8,000 + 700
9. twenty-four
10. seven hundred twenty-six

Reteach 2, page 60
1. 54,382
2. 26,502
3. 8,976
4. 12,090
5. 42,438; forty-two thousand, four hundred thirty-eight
6. 9,353; nine thousand, three hundred fifty-three
7. 27,000; twenty-seven thousand
8. 20,000 + 5,000 + 400 + 30 + 2
9. 60,000 + 4,000 + 800 + 90

Reteach 3, page 61
1. thousand
2. five hundred sixty-two; one hundred three
3. sixteen thousand, eight hundred twelve
4. nine thousand, one hundred
5. thirty-seven thousand, three hundred sixty
6. one hundred eighty-three thousand, four
7. three hundred sixty-two thousand, five hundred forty
8. nine hundred forty-five thousand, two hundred fifty-one

Reteach 4, page 62
1. <
2. >
3. >
4. >
5. >
6. <
7. <

(Reteach 4 continued)
8. >
9. >
10. >

Reteach 5, page 63
1. 400
2. 300
3. 300
4. 500
5. 900
6. 900
7. 300
8. 100
9. 6,000
10. 3,000
11. 2,000
12. 3,570
13. 1,200
14. 7,250
15. 2,510
16. 3,750

Reteach 6, page 64
1. millions
2. thousands
3. millions
4. ones
5. millions
6. ones
7. thousands
8. millions
9. million; thousand
10. million; thousand
11. million; thousand
12. one million, five hundred sixty-three thousand
13. five hundred fifty-five million
14. eighty-two million, seven hundred thousand, four
15. 2,121,000
16. 19,000,194
17. 108,045,010

Reteach 7, page 65
1. 3,070,000
2. 93,000
3. 1,900,000
4. 2,700,000
5. 355,000
6. 870,000
7. 10,482,800; 10,483,000
8. 3,709,800; 3,710,000
9. 253,893,600; 253,894,000
10. 512,746,300; 512,746,000
11. 59,974,100; 59,974,000
12. hundred thousands

(Reteach 7 continued)
13. thousands
14. ten thousands

Reteach 8, page 66
1. 4; 3
2. 8
3. 7
4. 3; 2; 6; 5; 9; 9
5. 5; 10; 13; 13
6. 5; 4; 8; 8

Reteach 9, page 67
1. 10; 10; 3; 7
2. 8
3. 6
4. 9
5. 7; 7
6. 11; 11
7. 11; 3
8. 9; 2
9. 5; 2
10. 7; 6
11. −; +
12. +; −
13. +; −
14. c
15. d
16. b
17. a

Reteach 10, page 68
1. False.
2. True.
3. open
4. False.
5. open
6. False.
7. False.
8. True.
9. 3
10. 9
11. 3
12. 8
13. 2
14. 4
15. 2
16. 10

Reteach 11, page 69
1. 40
2. 700
3. 4,000
4. 300; 900
5. 100; 400
6. 700; 1,000
7. 100; 600; 700

(Reteach 11 continued)
8. 400; 300; 0
9. 900; 600; 1,500
10. 2,000; 1,000; 1,000
11. 4,000; 2,000; 2,000
12. 7,000; 3,000; 4,000

Reteach 12, page 70
1. $10, $15, $16, $16.25
2. $.50, $.75, $.85, $.95, $.96, $.97, $.98
3. $.40; $.46, greater
4. $5.85, greater; $3.67
5. $14.05; $19.55, greater

Reteach 13, page 71
1. $1.50, $1.75, $2
2. $6.80, $6.90, $7, $8, $9, $10
3. $.20
4. $2.24
5. $7.15

Reteach 14, page 72
1. 5; 5; 15; 3; 15; 5; 15
2. 6; 6; 24; 6; 24; 6; 24
3. 7; 21; 3; 21; 3 × 7; 21
4. 3; 3; 3; 3; 3; 15; 5 × 3; 15
5. 16; 4 × 4 = 16
6. 9; 3 × 3 = 9
7. 28; 4 × 7 = 28
8. 25; 5 × 5 = 25
9. 18; 3 × 6 = 18
10. 12; 2 × 6 = 12

Reteach 15, page 73
1. 3; 18; 18; 3; 3; 18; 18; 3
2. 15; 5; 5; 15; 15; 3
3. 21; 3; 7; 21; 21 ÷ 7 = 3
4. 9; 5; 45; 9; 45; 45 ÷ 9 = 5
5. 32; 32 ÷ 4 = 8; 4 × 8 = 32; 32 ÷ 8 = 4
6. 2; 12 ÷ 2 = 6; 6 × 2 = 12; 2 × 6 = 12
7. 7; 63 ÷ 7 = 9; 7 × 9 = 63; 9 × 7 = 63
8. 14; 7 × 2 = 14; 14 ÷ 7 = 2; 14 ÷ 2 = 7

Reteach 16, page 74
1. 5
2. 6
3. 4
4. 5
5. 9 × 7

224

Answer Key • Reteach Worksheets

(Reteach 16 continued)

6. 5×6
7. 2
8. 4
9. 6
10. 4
11. 5×2
12. $5 \times 2; 30$
13. 2×6
14. 2×8

Reteach 17, page 75

1. $5.64
2. $17.80
3. $8.94
4. $13.11
5. $2.34
6. $1.72
7. $7.72
8. $11.85
9. $2.52
10. $2.45
11. $13.14
12. $13.52

Reteach 18, page 76

1. 1; 1
2. 2; 2
3. 2; 2
4. 1; 1
5. 2; 2
6. 2; 2
7. 800
8. 1,500
9. 2,400
10. 82,000

Reteach 19, page 77

1. 50
2. 50
3. 30; 40
4. 50; 30
5. 40; 800
6. 50; 70; 3,500
7. 70; 90; 6,300
8. 90; 50; 4,500
9. 40; 20; 800
10. 90; 80; 7,200
11. 40; 30; 1,200
12. 70; 20; 1,400

Reteach 20, page 78

1. 8; 4; 0; 3
2. $18 \div 9 = 2$
3. $32 \div 8 = 4$
4. $18 \div 6 = 3$
5. 6

(Reteach 20 continued)

6. 4
7. 9
8. 7
9. 7
10. 9
11. 6
12. 2
13. 7
14. 8
15. 3
16. 7
17. 5
18. 9
19. 1

Reteach 21, page 79

1. 6, 6
2. $35 \div 5 = 7, 7$
3. 1
4. 0
5. 9
6. 1
7. 8
8. 0
9. 9
10. 8
11. 6
12. 3
13. 7
14. 1

Reteach 22, page 80

1. 6; 12
2. 4; 13
3. 8; 17
4. 21
5. 4; 3
6. 7; 56
7. 2; 5
8. 3; 15
9. 5; 30
10. 10
11. 6
12. 9
13. 3
14. 5
15. 17
16. 8
17. 4
18. 18

Reteach 23, page 81

1. 3 R1
2. 2 R2
3. 3 R1
4. 3 R3
5. 5 R1

(Reteach 23 continued)

6. 4 R3
7. 6 R3
8. 9 R2
9. 6 R3
10. 8 R1
11. 7 R1
12. 3 R1
13. 7 R2
14. 4 R2
15. 4 R2
16. 5 R6

Reteach 24, page 82

1. 16 R1
2. 12 R1
3. 21 R2
4. 38 R1
5. 13 R4
6. 23 R3
7. 31 R1
8. 17 R3
9. 16 R4
10. 18 R1
11. 27 R1
12. 15 R3

Reteach 25, page 83

1. 151 R2
2. 132
3. 162 R1
4. 123
5. 131 R1
6. 124 R1
7. 128 R1
8. 153
9. 243 R3

Reteach 26, page 84

1. 209
2. 80 R2
3. 109 R2
4. 108 R5
5. 73 R2
6. 190 R3
7. 106 R2
8. 205 R3
9. 130 R3

Reteach 27, page 85

1. $1.21
2. $.89
3. $.19
4. $1.19
5. $3.05
6. $.13
7. $2.61

(Reteach 27 continued)

8. $2.32
9. $4.07

Reteach 28, page 86

1. 16
2. 240
3. 184
4. 148
5. 336
6. 416
7. Yes.
8. 15, Yes.
9. 8, No.
10. 8, No.
11. 18, 80, 140
12. 120, 92
13. yes, yes, yes
14. no, yes, yes
15. no, yes, yes
16. no, yes, no

Reteach 29, page 87

1. 945 R1
2. 626 R1
3. 963 R1
4. 804 R7
5. 965 R3
6. 516 R1
7. 920 R2
8. 709
9. 958 R4

Reteach 30, page 88

1. 7
2. 11
3. 23
4. 20
5. 49
6. 13
7. 12
8. 38
9. 71

Reteach 31, page 89

1. $\frac{3}{4} < \frac{4}{4}$
2. $\frac{1}{6} < \frac{2}{6}$
3. $\frac{3}{5} > \frac{2}{5}$
4. $\frac{3}{4} > \frac{2}{4}$
5. $\frac{3}{6} < \frac{5}{6}$
6. $\frac{3}{3} > \frac{1}{3}$
7. $\frac{1}{15} < \frac{4}{5}$

Answer Key • Reteach Worksheets

(Reteach 31 continued)

8. $\frac{5}{6} > \frac{4}{6}$

9. $\frac{4}{4} > \frac{2}{4}$

10. $\frac{3}{6} > \frac{1}{6}$

Reteach 32, page 90

1. $\frac{2}{4}, \frac{3}{6}, \frac{4}{8}$

2. $\frac{4}{6}$

3. $\frac{6}{8}$

4. $\frac{2}{6}$

5. $\frac{2}{2}, \frac{3}{3}, \frac{4}{4}, \frac{5}{5}, \frac{6}{6}$

6. $\frac{0}{2}, \frac{0}{3}, \frac{0}{4}, \frac{0}{6}, \frac{0}{8}$

Reteach 33, page 91

1. is less than
2. is greater than
3. $\frac{1}{8} < \frac{6}{8}$
4. $\frac{2}{2} > \frac{1}{2}$
5. $\frac{3}{4} > \frac{2}{4}$
6. $\frac{2}{4} > \frac{1}{4}$
7. $\frac{3}{8} < \frac{5}{8}$
8. $\frac{4}{8} = \frac{2}{4}$
9. $\frac{7}{8} < \frac{2}{2}$
10. $\frac{3}{4} = \frac{6}{8}$
11. $\frac{1}{8}, \frac{2}{8}, \frac{4}{8}, \frac{7}{8}, \frac{8}{8}$
12. $\frac{0}{4}, \frac{1}{4}, \frac{2}{4}, \frac{3}{4}$

Reteach 34, page 92

1.
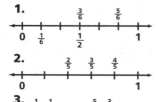

2.

3.

(Reteach 34 continued)

4.–5.
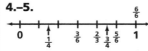

Reteach 35, page 93

1. open
2. closed
3. closed
4. open
5. Yes.
6. No.
7. Yes.
8. No.
9. triangle
10. rectangle
11. triangle
12. square

Reteach 36, page 94

1. point
2. line segment
3. line
4. line segment
5.–8. Check students' drawings.
9. perpendicular
10. parallel

Reteach 37, page 95

1. $\overrightarrow{EF}$
2. $\angle QRS$
3. $\angle RST$
4. $\overrightarrow{DE}$
5. Yes.
6. No.
7. No.
8. Yes.

Reteach 38, page 96

1. No.
2. Yes.
3. Yes.
4. No.
5. c
6. a
7. c

Reteach 39, page 97

1. right
2. acute
3. obtuse
4. obtuse
5. acute
6. right
7. acute
8. right
9. obtuse

Reteach 40, page 98

1. radius
2. diameter
3. radius
4. diameter
5. half turn
6. three-quarter turn
7. full turn
8. one-quarter turn

Reteach 41, page 99

1. No.
2. Yes.
3. Yes.
4. No.
5. Yes.
6. Yes.
7. No.
8. No.
9. Yes.
10. No.
11. Yes.
12. No.

Reteach 42, page 100

1. isosceles
2. equilateral
3. scalene
4. scalene
5. equilateral
6. isosceles
7. equilateral
8. scalene
9. isosceles
10. scalene
11. isosceles
12. equilateral

Reteach 43, page 101

1. triangle
2. pentagon
3. hexagon
4. quadrilateral
5. square
6. trapezoid

(Reteach 43 continued)

7. rhombus
8. rectangle
9. trapezoid
10. rectangle
11. square
12. rhombus

Reteach 44, page 102

1. sphere; 0
2. cylinder; 2
3. rectangular prism; 6
4. cube; 6
5. rectangular pyramid; 5
6. cone; 1

Reteach 45, page 103

Check students' space figures.

Reteach 46, page 104

1. $4\frac{1}{2}$
2. 3; 3
3. $2; 2\frac{1}{2}; 2\frac{1}{2}$
4. $2\frac{1}{2}; 3; 3$

Reteach 47, page 105

1. 16
2. 18
3. 16
4. 24
5. 20
6. 24
7. 24
8. 26

Reteach 48, page 106

1. 9
2. 12
3. 16
4. 15
5. 8
6. 12
7. 10
8. 6
9. 19

Reteach 49, page 107

1. 32
2. 3; 24
3. 9; 3; 27
4. 15; 3; 45
5. 4; 4; 16
6. 12; 2; 24

Answer Key • Reteach Worksheets

Reteach 50, page 108

1. 4
2. 2
3. 15
4. 41
5. 30
6. 10; 40
7. 6; 60
8. 8; 10; 80
9. 50
10. 90
11. 20
12. 70

Reteach 51, page 109

1. 10 m
2. 10 km
3. 10 cm
4. 80
5. 7,000
6. 5; 500
7. 4; 10; 40
8. 4
9. 8
10. 9
11. 4
12. 30
13. 5,000
14. 300
15. 70
16. 5,000
17. 30,000

Reteach 52, page 110

1. smaller; more
2. larger; fewer
3. larger; fewer
4. smaller; more
5. 4,000
6. $1\frac{1}{2}$
7. $2\frac{1}{2}$
8. 3,500
9. $4\frac{1}{2}$
10. 8
11. 3
12. 9,000
13. 1,500
14. $5\frac{1}{2}$
15. 8
16. 6,000

Reteach 53, page 111

1. cooler
2. cooler
3. warmer
4. 19°C
5. 32°C
6. 29°C
7. 4°C
8. 15°C
9. 9°C

Reteach 54, page 112

1. 2 in.
2. $1\frac{1}{2}$ in.
3. $1\frac{3}{4}$ in.
4. $\frac{3}{4}$ in.
5. $2\frac{1}{4}$ in.
6. $2\frac{3}{4}$ in.
7. c
8. d
9. a
10. b

Reteach 55, page 113

1. 4 miles
2. 4 feet
3. 4 yards
4. feet
5. yards
6. miles
7. miles
8. yards
9. feet
10. feet
11. 36
12. 48
13. 2
14. 2
15. 2
16. 60
17. 6
18. 4
19. 84

Reteach 56, page 114

1. 12, 14, 16; 5, 6, 7, 8
2. 40, 48, 56, 64; 20, 24, 28, 32; 4, 5, 6, 7, 8
3. 1
4. 4
5. 16
6. 5, 6; 64, 80, 96
7. 16

(Reteach 56 continued)

8. 32
9. 3

Reteach 57, page 115

1. 25°F
2. −6°F
3. 16°F
4. 32°F
5. 7°F
6. −5°F
7. −20°F
8. 0°F
9. −10°F
10. b
11. b
12. b
13. 90°F; beach
14. 25°F; colder
15. 0°F
16. −10°F

Reteach 58, page 116

1. 24; 24 yd
2. 24; 24 in.
3. 28; 28 cm
4. 21 m

Reteach 59, page 117

1. 18; 18
2. 16; 16
3. 20 square m
4. 9 square cm
5. 108 square dm, 108 square dm
6. 144 square dm, 144 square dm
7. 84 square cm
8. 81 square m

Reteach 60, page 118

1. 22
2. 16
3. 16 cm; 14 square cm
4. 22 km; 19 square km

Reteach 61, page 119

1. 36; 24; 48; 108 square ft
2. 4; 4; 96; 96 square yd
3. 82 square in.
4. 54 square in.

Reteach 62, page 120

1. 8; 8 cubic cm
2. 5; 2; 30; 30 cubic cm
3. 27 cubic cm

(Reteach 62 continued)

4. 24 cubic cm
5. 16 cubic cm
6. 24 cubic cm

Reteach 63, page 121

1. $\frac{9}{10}$; 0.9
2. four tenths; $\frac{4}{10}$; 0.4
3. two tenths; $\frac{2}{10}$; 0.2
4. eight tenths; $\frac{8}{10}$; 0.8
5. three tenths; $\frac{3}{10}$; 0.3
6. seven tenths; $\frac{7}{10}$; 0.7
7. one tenth; $\frac{1}{10}$; 0.1
8. five tenths; $\frac{5}{10}$; 0.5

Reteach 64, page 122

1. $2\frac{4}{10}$; 2.4
2. $1\frac{9}{10}$; 1.9
3. $2\frac{6}{10}$; 2.6
4. 0.5
5. 1.4
6. 2.3
7. 0.8
8. 3.1
9. 2.7
10. $\frac{9}{10}$
11. $2\frac{4}{10}$
12. $1\frac{5}{10}$
13. $3\frac{3}{10}$
14. $2\frac{8}{10}$
15. $4\frac{9}{10}$

Reteach 65, page 123

1. e
2. d
3. b
4. f
5. a
6. c
7. 0.8; $\frac{8}{10}$
8. 2.3; $2\frac{3}{10}$
9. 4.04; $4\frac{4}{100}$
10. 0.07; $\frac{7}{100}$

Answer Key • Reteach Worksheets

(Reteach 65 continued)

11. $0.14; \frac{14}{100}$

12. $3.06; 3\frac{6}{100}$

13. fifteen hundredths

14. three and thirty-five hundredths

Reteach 66, page 124

1. 0.40
2. 0.6
3. 0.9
4. 1.50
5. 3.8
6. 8.3
7. <
8. =
9. <
10. >
11. <
12. >

Reteach 67, page 125

1. $\frac{5}{10}$

2. $\frac{75}{100}$

3. $\frac{2}{10}$

4. $\frac{4}{100}$

5. $\frac{35}{100}$

6. $\frac{8}{100}$

7. 2.5
8. 1.75
9. 3.8
10. 0.8
11. 0.18
12. 5.15

Reteach 68, page 126

1. 58 and 59
2. 91 and 92
3. 23 and 24
4. 15 and 16
5. 24
6. 84
7. 17
8. 7
9. 187
10. 218
11. 79
12. 456
13. 23.9
14. 84.0
15. 16.8
16. 0.3

(Reteach 68 continued)

17. 186.8
18. 218.5
19. 79.1
20. 456

Reteach 69, page 127

1. 9.44
2. 9.82
3. 8.18
4. 7.29
5. 8.15
6. 8.78
7. 6.95
8. 7.3
9. 9.97

Reteach 70, page 128

1. 1.62
2. 7.18
3. 5.06
4. 0.77
5. 1.14
6. 2.34
7. 2.84
8. 1.59
9. 2.02

Reteach 71, page 129

1. 37 R2
2. 24 R6
3. 49 R3
4. 63 R2
5. 77 R2
6. 94
7. 35 R2
8. 61 R5
9. 59
10. 87 R3
11. 46
12. 58 R2

Reteach 72, page 130

1. 800; 8,000
2. 150; 1,500; 15,000
3. 24; 240; 2,400; 24,000
4. 20; 200; 2,000; 20,000
5. 42; 420; 4,200; 42,000
6. 27; 270; 2,700; 27,000
7. 560
8. 3,000
9. 14,000
10. 2,800
11. 100
12. 480
13. 32,000
14. 3,600

(Reteach 72 continued)

15. 36,000

Reteach 73, page 131

1. 6 R8
2. 4 R5
3. 1 R45
4. 4 R15
5. 1 R19
6. 3 R16
7. 4 R11
8. 3 R14

Reteach 74, page 132

1. 2 R18
2. 3 R1
3. 2 R23
4. 5 R2

Reteach 75, page 133

1. 6 R17
2. 9 R4
3. 4 R12
4. 9 R17
5. 9 R45
6. 2 R29
7. 1 R40
8. 6

Reteach 76, page 134

1. 24 R9
2. Estimate: 20; Answer: 23
3. Estimate: 10;
Answer: 11 R47
4. Estimate: 24;
Answer: 24 R6
5. Estimate: 15;
Answer: 15 R4
6. Estimate: 30; Answer: 32

Reteach 77, page 135

1. 10 R6
2. Estimate: 19;
Answer: 20 R13
3. Estimate: 30; Answer: 30
4. Estimate: 20;
Answer: 20 R13
5. Estimate: 10;
Answer: 10 R27
6. Estimate: 20;
Answer: 20 R5

Reteach 78, page 136

1. 42 R34
2. 62 R13
3. 58 R32

(Reteach 78 continued)

4. 72 R4
5. 24 R6
6. 32 R14

Reteach 79, page 137

1. 40 R14
2. 52 R15

Compatible numbers may vary for 3–6.

3. $30 \times 4 = 120$; 4
4. $20 \times 70 = 1,400$; 77 R9
5. $50 \times 30 = 1,500$; 32 R14
6. $60 \times 3 = 180$; 3 R6

Reteach 80, page 138

1. dog weights
2. weight in pounds
3. 40 pounds
4. 70 pounds
5. See graph below.

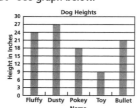

Reteach 81, page 139

1. 3
2. 5
3. See plot line below.

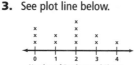

Reteach 82, page 140

1. Telephone calls made last week.
2. Each symbol stands for 5 telephone calls.
3. Ian, Janet, and Nick
4. Leroy
5. 20
6. Wendy
7. Sara, with 3 telephone icons.

Reteach 83, page 141

1. spittlebug
2. 2
3. squash bug and cinch bug
4. 18

Answer Key • Reteach Worksheets

(Reteach 83 continued)

5. $\frac{6}{18} = \frac{1}{3}$
6. stinkbug
7. less than $\frac{1}{4}$ of the votes
8. cinch bug and squash bug

Reteach 84, page 142

1. See table below.

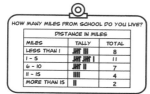

2. 32
3. 4
4. 8
5. 1–5 miles from school; 4 more
6. 6
7. Answers may vary.

Reteach 85, page 143

1. See line plot below.

2. 8
3. $10 - 4 = 6$
4. Yes; 4
5. 8
6. mode 9; median 8; range 6

Reteach 86, page 144

1. age in days
2. height in inches
3. 21 days
4. between 21 days and 28 days
5. $10 - 1 = 9$
6. Possible answer: increase; the seedling still seems to be growing.
7. See graph below.

Reteach 87, page 145

1. red, yellow, green
2. green
3. 3, 10
4. 6, 10
5. Possible answer: red, because the greatest number of balls in the jar are red.
6. 1, 2, 3
7. 2, 6
8. 1

Reteach 88, page 146

1. 2
2. red, green, blue
3. green
4. $\frac{4}{9}$
5. $\frac{4}{9} + \frac{2}{9} = \frac{6}{9}$ or $\frac{2}{3}$
6. 3, 9
7. $\frac{2}{9}$
8. a red marble
9. $\frac{2}{9} + \frac{3}{9} = \frac{5}{9}$

Reteach 89, page 147

1. heads, tails
2. 1, 2, 3, 4, 5, 6
3. 12
4. blue, red
5. small, medium, large, extra-large
6. See diagram below.

Color		Size
red		S M L XL
blue		S M L XL

Reteach 90, page 148

1. D
2. C; 0, 4, 2
3. B
4. A
5. (6, 1)
6. (1, 5); 1, 5

Reteach 91, page 149

1. a; $\times$; $7 \times a$ or $a \times 7$
2. $9 + c$ or $c + 9$
3. $c + 2$
4. c
5. e
6. f
7. a
8. b
9. h
10. d
11. g

Reteach 92, page 150

1. 4; 4
2. 3; 3
3. 7; 2
4. 6; 6
5. 5
6. 8
7. 2
8. 5

Reteach 93, page 151

1. the number of people in the theater; p; $p - 15$; $p - 15 = 82$
2. $a \div 6$; $a \div 6 = 8$
3. $b + 12 = 29$
4. $b \times 10 = 120$
5. $k - 8 = 9$
6. $45 \div p = 5$
7. $n + 33 = 91$

Reteach 94, page 152

1. 8; 8; table: 12
2. $7; profit; $7 = p$; table: $7
3. 11; $t \times 11 = p$; table: 44
4. The number of singles divided by 2 equals the number of pairs; $s \div 2 = p$; table: 5

Reteach 95, page 153

1. R
2. 0; 3; 1; T
3. P
4. Q
5. S
6. (0, 5)
7. 1; 2; (1, 2)
8. (3, 3)
9. (4, 6)
10. (5, 0)

Reteach 96, page 154

1.–14.

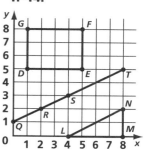

2. 5; 5
5. rectangle *DEFG*
10. a line
14. a triangle

Reteach 97, page 155

1. $y = 2$; (4, 2); $y = 3$; (6, 3)

x	x ÷ 2	y	Ordered Pair (x, y)
2	2 ÷ 2	1	(2, 1)
4	4 ÷ 2	2	(4, 2)
6	6 ÷ 2	3	(6, 3)
8	8 ÷ 2	4	(8, 4)
10	10 ÷ 2	5	(10, 5)

2.

x	x + 3	y	Ordered Pair (x, y)
0	0 + 3	3	(0, 3)
1	1 + 3	4	(1, 4)
2	2 + 3	5	(2, 5)
3	3 + 3	6	(3, 6)
4	4 + 3	7	(4, 7)

3. a line
4. a line

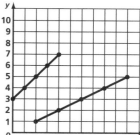

Answer Key • Extension Worksheets

Extension 1, page 159

1. True.
2. False.
3. False.
4. True.
5. True.
6. Some of the diamonds are plain.
7. Some of the figures with stripes are triangles.
8. True.
9. None of the triangles are plain.

Extension 2, page 160

1. 1 + 1 + 1 = 3
2. 5 + 1 + 1 = 7
3. 10 − 1 = 9
4. 10 + 10 + 1 + 1 = 22
5. 50 − 10 = 40
6. 50 + 10 + 10 = 70
7. 50 + 1 = 51
8. 50 + 10 + 1 + 1 = 62
9. 500 + 100 = 600
10. 100 − 10 + 5 = 95
11. 50 + 10 + 10 + 5 = 75
12. 100 + 50 − 10 = 140
13. XVII
14. XLV
15. LIV
16. LXXXI
17. CII
18. MD
19. CCL
20. MDC

Extension 3, page 161

1. 26
2. 35
3. 64
4. 46
5. 76
6. 25
7. 73
8. 94
9. 88
10. 39
11. 15
12. 58
13. 1,138
14. 898
15. 685
16. 333
17. 132
18. 242
19. 6,585
20. 7,338

(Extension 3 continued)
21. 1,022
22. 2,129

Extension 4, page 162

1. row 4 −3, 1;
   row 5 −1, 6, 4, 1;
   row 6 −1, 5, 10, 10, 5, 1
2. 3, 3
3. added 1 + 4 and 4 + 1
4. 1, 6, 15, 20, 15, 6, 1
5. 1, 7, 21, 35, 35, 21, 7, 1
6. 1, 2, 4, 8, 16, 32; The sum of each row is double the sum of the row above it.
7. Answers will vary. Possible answers include: A diagonal pattern beginning in row 2 is counting by ones. A diagonal pattern beginning in row 3 is +2, +3, +4, +5, +6, and so on.

Extension 5, page 163

1.

	30	7
20	20 × 30 = 600	20 × 7 = 140
4	4 × 30 = 120	4 × 7 = 28

600 + 140 + 120 + 28 = 888

2.

	40	2
50	2,000	100
9	360	18

2,000 + 100 + 360 + 18 = 2,478

3.

	40	8
80	3,200	640
4	160	32

3,200 + 640 + 160 + 32 = 4,032

4.

	20	3
40	40 × 20 = 800	40 × 3 = 120
6	6 × 20 = 120	6 × 20 = 18

46 × 23 = 1,058

5.

	50	7
20	20 × 50 = 1,000	20 × 7 = 140
3	3 × 50 = 150	3 × 7 = 21

23 × 57 = 1,311

Extension 6, page 164

1. the product of 3 and 2 subtracted from 9, or 3; the difference of 9 and 3 multiplied by 2, or 12
2. the quotient 24 divided by 6 minus 3, or 1; 24 divided by the difference of 6 and 3, or 8
3. the sum of 18 and 2 multiplied by the difference of 5 and 4, or 20
4. 8 × 4 − 8
5. 72 ÷ (28 − 16)
6. (21 + 9) × 3
7. (16 − 8) × 2 + 6

Extension 7, page 165

1.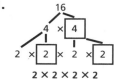
2 × 2 × 2 × 2

2.
2 × 3 × 5

3.
2 × 3 × 7

4.
2 × 2 × 5

5.
3 × 3 × 3

6.
2 × 2 × 7

(Extension 7 continued)

7.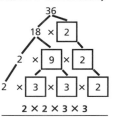
2 × 2 × 3 × 3

8.
2 × 2 × 2 × 2 × 3

Extension 8, page 166

1. 6
2. 12
3. 3
4. 6
5. 9
6. 12
7. 2
8. 4
9. 8
10. 3; 3
11. 3; 3; 12; 12

Extension 9, page 167

1. flip
2. slide
3. neither flip nor slide
4. flip
5.–7. Check students' drawings.

Extension 10, page 168

1. similar
2. similar
3. similar
4. not similar
5. Check students' drawings.

Extension 11, page 169

1. True; all squares have 4 right angles and 4 sides.
2. False; in a rectangle all the sides may not be the same length.
3. True; all rhombi have 2 pairs of parallel sides.
4. False; all parallelograms do not have 4 right angles

Answer Key • Extension Worksheets

(Extension 11 continued)

5. True; a trapezoid has exactly 1 pair of parallel sides and a parallelogram must have exactly 2 pairs of parallel sides.
6. True; all squares are quadrilaterals with 4 congruent sides.

Extension 12, page 170

1. 10:00 A.M.
2. 12:00 noon
3. 8:00 A.M.
4. 12:00 noon
5. 11:00 A.M.
6. 11:00 A.M.
7. 9:00 A.M.
8. 10:00 A.M.
9. 1:00 P.M.
10. 12:00 noon
11. 1:00 P.M.

Extension 13, page 171

1. 5 cm; 5 km
2. 7 cm; 7 km
3. 7 cm; 7 km
4. 2 cm; 4 km
5. 4 cm; 8 km
6. 8 cm; 16 km
7. 9 cm; 18 km
8. 3 cm; 6 km
9. 11 cm; 22 km
10. 13 cm; 26 km

Extension 14, page 172

1. 2; 2; $\frac{4}{10}$; 0.4
2. 5; 5; $\frac{45}{100}$; 0.45
3. 0.75
4. 0.6
5. 0.32
6. 0.78
7. 0.48
8. 0.85
9. <
10. <
11. >

Extension 15, page 173

1. 156 R3
2. 113 R5
3. 239 R1
4. 175 R1
5. 162 R1
6. 118 R2
7. 103 R4

(Extension 15 continued)

8. 117 R3
9. 253
10. 328 R3
11. 211 R2
12. 494 R3
13.

Quotient	10	8	5	7	4	11	3	4
Divisor	8	8	8	8	8	8	9	9
Dividend	82	65	43	58	36	94	29	39
Remainder	2	1	3	2	4	6	2	3

Extension 16, page 174

1. 760 R2
2. 758 R16
3. 217 R54
4. 248 R2
5. 404 R29
6. 998 R19
7. 914 R7
8. 895 R21
9. 515 R9
10. 801
11. 790 R17
12. 893 R33

Extension 17, page 175

1. adult attendance
2. Saturday
3. Thursday
4. Check students' graphs.

Extension 18, page 176

1.–2. Check students' graphs.
3. In August, the two lines intersect at 12; the two girls had the same number of stuffed animals.
4. Angela had 12 more stuffed animals in June.
5. Carol had 11 more stuffed animals in October.
6. The number of stuffed animals in Carol's collection is growing each month, while Angela's collection is getting smaller.

Extension 19, page 177

1. See diagram below.

Stem	Leaves
1	8 9
2	2 3 5 6 6 7 8 9
3	0 2 3 4 5 7 8
4	0 2 4 8
5	1

2. 18
3. 51
4. 26
5. Most players are 20–29 years old.

Extension 20, page 178

1. <
2. <
3. >
4. >
5. <
6. <
7. >
8. >
9. >
10. <
11. >
12. >
13. $^-9$, $^-5$, $^-3$
14. 0, 4, 9
15. $^-6$, 3, 7
16. $^-10$, $^-5$, 5
17. any two digits from $^-8$ to $^-1$
18. any two digits from $^-3$ to 3
19. any two digits from $^-5$ to $^-1$
20. 7, 8